ANNIE MAE JOHNSON, CARY JOHNSON, CLI...
JOHNSON, CASSIE JOYCE, MIKI KAIPAKA, BERN...KANE, SUSAN KANE,
INESE KAUFMAN, KINKOS, INDU KLINE, ARNIE KOMITSKY, JOHN LAIR,
TONY LEROY, DOROTHY LEWIS, STEPHEN MAGNER, CAROLINE
MAPOTHER, JOHN MAURER, FRED MAYO, LYNN MAYO, BEN McDONALD,
HATTIE McGILL, ASHA McLAUGHLIN, MARK McLAUGHLIN, WILMA
MITCHELL, JOHNNIE MAE MONTGOMERY, PEGGY MORAN, ANNE
NASTOROWICZ, STEFAN NASTOROWICZ, EMILY NOBLE, HOLLY RALSTON
OYLER, BILL PARRISH, CATHERINE PARRISH, SUZANNE PARRISH, ANNA
PATTERSON, ANNA LOUISE PATTERSON, HENRY LEE PATTERSON, DEANNA
PELFREY, ANNE PEOPLES, THE PRASAD PROJECT, DEAN RAMSDEN, ALEX
RANKIN, ALEXANDER RANKIN, ED RANKIN, HUNTER RANKIN, JOHN
RANKIN, JULIAN RANKIN, MARTIE RANKIN, SARAH RANKIN, TAYLOR
RANKIN, TOM RANKIN, EVAN RAY, TRUDY RAY, MARTIN RAY, ELIZABETH
REINSTEDLER, FRANK RHODES, LISA RICHARDS, DOROTHY ROBERTSON,
ROXY, ELLIE SACHS, LEONARD SAPHIER, NATHAN SANGSTER, PAM
SATTERLY, JUDY SCHAFMAN, LARRY SCHAFMAN, NANCY SENNET, DAVID
SHULHAFER, DORIS SHUMAKE, REVEREND SHUMAKE, DERIK SHELOR,
BEVERLY SILVER, MONICA SMITH, SOUTH FALLSBURG POST OFFICE, JAN
SPILLER, JONATHAN STAR, STELLA, JESSE STOFF, JESSIE STUTTERS, LIZZIE
SUMMERS, JANE TATE, TOM TATE, VIRGINIA TATE, KATHY TAUSTINE,
TEDDY BUMPUS, LYNN TISZA, STEVE THOMPSON, T.L.E.T.C, KENDRA
TODD, RICK URSCHEL, VIDEOBRED, KAREN VOLEVIC, RON WAHL, EDIE
WELLS, PEYTON WELLS, CHARLEY WILLIAMS, MATTIE WILSON, JOAN
WINKLER, ANGELA WOODARD, MARY WOODARD, DONNA WOODS

Cookin' Up A Storm

Cookin' Up A Storm

THE LIFE AND RECIPES OF ANNIE JOHNSON

Jane Lee Rankin

GRACE PUBLISHERS
NEW YORK

Copyright © 1998 by Jane Lee Rankin

Printed in the United States of America
All Rights Reserved

First Edition
Rankin, Jane Lee, 1960–
        Cookin' up a storm: the life and recipes of Annie Johnson
        by Jane Lee Rankin.– 1st ed.
        p. cm.
        Includes index
        Preassigned LCCN:98-84673
        ISBN 0-9657387-0-1

        1. Cookery, American–Southern style. 2. Johnson, Annie, 1916–
        3. Afro-American cooks–Kentucky–Louisville–Biography. 4. Cooks–
        Kentucky–Louisville–Biography. I. Title. II. Title: Cookin' up a storm

        TX715.2.S68R36 1998   641.5'975
                                              QBI98-282

Grace Publishers, P.O. Box 769, South Fallsburg, NY 12779

For Annie, with all my love.

Acknowledgments

The process of researching, writing, editing, and publishing this book has been a profound journey. The inside front and back covers show the names of everyone to whom I am indebted: the friends and family members who lent their encouragement, the taste testers, the recipe reviewers, the editors, the photographers and videographers, and those who gave me their feedback. Thank you all for your love, support, and blessings.

My heart is filled with love for my mother, who died in 1986 and continues to be with me in so many ways; for my father, who allowed his sense of integrity and responsibility to rub off on me; and for the source of benevolent grace that flows through my life, making everything possible.

Jane Lee Rankin
March 1998

CONTENTS

FOREWARD

In my sermons and talks all over the world, I have stated that God's primary purpose in the enslavement of African-Americans in the United States was to teach America how to love. In the face of a host of unspeakable indignities, we kept faith in America. We worked the fields. We built the cities. We fought America's wars. We made cotton king. African American women nurtured white babies and cooked in white kitchens.

Annie Johnson was not a slave. She was perhaps the granddaughter of a slave. But she captured the love and behavior that enabled African American women to love unconditionally, to turn the other cheek and go the second mile. Annie is part of a unheralded institution of cooks and nannies in America. And Lee Rankin's *Cookin' Up a Storm: The Life and Recipes of Annie Johnson* rewards these beautiful women, members of this monumental institution, who gave so much to so many.

These women adorned the homes of prominent white families not only in the South but all along the East Coast. My mother was one of them. She was a live-in cook for a prominent family in Cambridge, Massachusetts, and Newport, Rhode Island.

Annie is not educated, at least not in academics, but she has great wisdom. God is the center of her life. Jesus is the joy of her being. It is this deep inner conviction and faith in God which makes Annie so wonderfully captivating. As Annie says, "Oh the Lord is so good. The Lord give you what you need."

Annie was the start of the Rankin morning. She was the one who saw that they not only ate well but that they could look to her to instill constructive values in the children's lives. She deeply loved the Rankins, and they deeply loved her. An honest appraisal of their relationship has to recognize that Annie could lift the love and vision of the Rankin family beyond the racism that permeated the time. Annie was their Annie. There was real love, deep respect, wholesome dependence and interaction. Annie did not just give. She received and continues to receive.

Most of Annie's recipes were stored in her head. The procedures went something like this: Some eggs, a bit of butter, throw in some sugar, a pinch of this and a pinch of that, keep stirring until you get the right blend, pour it in a pan, and put it in the oven until its done. Basically her cooking was a matter of the heart. Filled with the kind of magic which works miracles.

I love pies, especially lemon meringue pie. So I read and reread and read again the pie section. It took me back to the days in my mother's kitchen, watching her as she cooked. What a brainwashing this did for my imagination.

Thank you Lee Rankin for introducing America to your Annie and acknowledging the beautiful Annies of our nation! As she says in the book, "I feel like shoutin', I'm so happy!"

Dr. Eugene Callender

Former Senior Minister of Presbyterian Church of the Master in New York City

First Vice Chairperson for the National Center and Caucus for Black Aging

INTRODUCTION

Annie Johnson came into our lives when I was six weeks old. It was January of 1961 in my hometown of Louisville, Kentucky, and everyone in the family except my father had chicken pox. It was a crisis that needed a quick solution, and Annie was that solution.

My mother definitely needed Annie's help, with or without a chicken pox epidemic. Mother was not, to put it kindly, "domestically inclined," and had four children—three boys and me—all under the age of six. As Annie tells the story, we were a handful.

Annie started working one day a week, and before long she was with us all five weekdays. For over 25 years, Annie cooked the meals, cleaned the house, did the laundry, and helped my mother take care of us. Somewhere along the way, she became another member of the family, baking cakes on our birthdays and crying when we went away to school. She was one of my mother's closest friends and now has become one of mine.

Although Annie officially retired years ago, she remains very much a part of our family. We stay in touch by phone, send gifts back and forth, and go to visit her in her home. Her circle of birthday cake baking now includes the Rankin grandchildren, and she still spoils my father with stuffed green peppers and bean soup.

At age 81, Annie has rheumatoid arthritis, chronic lung problems, and a congestive heart condition. For the last six years she has not been able to go out in hot, cold, or humid weather. In spite of requiring breathing treatments, oxygen, and numerous medications, Annie continues to do what she can for others. She makes herself available as a source of comfort, support, and advice based on a lifetime of experience. As Annie puts it, "You know, I believe the reason I does so good is because I try. You gots to try. Do your part, and leave the rest to God."

Annie's greatest gifts to me over the years have been the examples of her own life and of her faith in God. Although life has been difficult at times, she is not bitter. I have seen her scared and I have seen her worried, but I have never seen her doubt God's love and presence in her life. Her heart is full of love for God and for the people around her. She lives with God as her companion.

The more I think about Annie, the more I see and appreciate her special contribution to my life. When I look at my own life, I see the impact of her example and values in so many ways. The idea for this book sprang from those realizations. I was inspired to create a tribute to Annie, a record of her story and a record of her recipes—because it is through her food that Annie is able to communicate with virtually everyone. When I shared the idea with others, I received support and encouragement. Touched by Annie's story, some even shed tears at the memory of someone who played a similar role in their life.

As the idea for this book—a cookbook to honor Annie and to celebrate her cooking and her life—developed, I realized it would be necessary for me to confront the difference in our race head-on, since I am white and Annie is black. I do not want (nor am I qualified) to make this book about the social, political, or racial issues, nor do I want to innocently offend anyone by glossing over them as they relate to this book. I am sensitive to the disrespectful treatment African Americans have received in life and in art. Further, I can attribute much of my sensitivity to the special relationship I am blessed to have with Annie. I can state, honestly and from the heart, that Annie is quite simply one of the warmest, most loving, and wisest individuals it has been my privilege to know. My only intentions in writing this book are to honor, celebrate, and acknowledge Annie.

Annie has a lot of things to say about quite a number of topics, and she does not require my assistance to say them. It was my choice to let Annie speak for herself—not only in her own words but in her own dialect. What Annie has to say—and how she says it—are equally vital to understanding Annie's message.

In the process of creating this book, my relationship with Annie has grown deeper and stronger. While working on the book, in the spring 1997, I was diagnosed with breast cancer. Though shaken by this news, I found comfort in Annie's example. I had been by her side as she faced threats to her own health, and I was inspired by her acceptance of God's will. As my outer life was thrown into turmoil, inside I found that I was steady, calm, and filled with faith. The same qualities I admire in Annie were coming to life in me.

I have three prayers for this book. First, that the book communicate Annie's rich experience in life. Second, that Annie be acknowledged and remembered for who she is and her special contribution. And last, that like me, you will be moved by Annie's example. Perhaps we all will be inspired to be more like her.

Annie and Lee

ANNIE
On Coming Up the Hard Way

I was born on the Fourth of July, 1916, in Chambers County, Alabama.
My mama, she was Addie Bailey, 'fore she married my daddy, Carol Dawson.
I was born at home with a midwife. I was the onliest child, and I weren't
spoil't either.

I was real young when Daddy died. I don't know how ol' he was. I 'member
him, but I still don't 'member his age. Unh hunh. You know, like they talk
about "breathin' problems" you can get? Now they calls it "asthma." That's
what was wrong—he couldn't get his breath. And, see, they didn't have nothin'
for that back then. Leastways, not where we was livin'.

I was born in Alabama at my grandmother's farm, right across't the border
from West Point, Georgia. My grandmother was a sharecropper and a former
slave. She treated me very strict, and she weren't 'fraid to give me a hard
whuppin'. Maybe that was 'causin' the way she come up during slavery—I can't
really say. I didn't like it none at the time, but later I appreciated being raised
up strict like that. That's how come I was able to build up a strong character.

My grandfather was there in the big ol' farmhouse with us for a while, but he
died. My uncle and his wife, and my other two uncles—they wasn't married—
they all was there, and my auntie and my mother. That's the reason I had to
make so many biscuits. Ever' mornin' from the time I turned ten, I got up at
four o'clock to cook breakfast so they could go to field.

We'd bake our cakes and pies a week ahead of time and put apples all around
'em and then put 'em in the drawers. They was good. You could smell them
things, I don't know how far off.

My mother would cut wood and carry it to town and sell it for a dollar and a
half a load. And I would pick blackberries and take 'em to town and sell 'em.
I'd carry 'em eight miles on my head—in a pan, in a basket, anythin'. Wouldn't
even fall off, jus' set right there on my head. I bet I couldn't do that now.
Used to sell them blackberries for ten cents a quart. We sold everthin' we
could from the garden.

I'd get to go to town to help carry in our last bales of cotton. I'd be sittin' there up on top of the wagon, on top of them bales of cotton. And if you'd go out in the field and scrape some cotton that was left over, you could sell it. They let you sell it and get the money. It wouldn't be that much, maybe thirty or forty cent. But in them days you'd a thought you had a hundred dollars. Yeah!

When my grandmother would milk the cow, I'd have to hold on to the cow's calf—the calf be wantin' to get at that milk, too. When you milkin' the cow, the strippins comes out last. We took an old butter churn to the strippins and made our own butter. We didn't waste nothin'.

We'd milk the cow for our milk and butter. We'd pick the cotton and take it to the gin. We'd raise up the corn, mill it, and feed the family wit' it. We'd pick peanuts off the vine, let 'em dry, then shell 'em and eat 'em. Everthin' you goes to the store for now, we had right there in the field. It was truly a blessin'.

On a Saturday, we'd work half a day in the field and we'd come home and scrub the floors with a shuck mop. We'd sprinkle sand on the floor for soap powder and scrub it. Then we'd get that sand off and rinse it. That wood floor was just as clean and white—oh, it was so pretty! Then we'd wash up and get ready for Sunday.

Sunday mornin', we'd get up and start a big dinner for after church. We walked eight miles on the country road into town for church—Saint John the Baptist Church. Reverend King was my pastor. He was from Atlanta, Georgia.

I didn't get a chance to go to school that much, 'causin' I had to go to field. In August, 'round the time to pick cotton, I didn't get to go to school much at all. When I did go to school, I didn't have much time to study or nothin'. A lot of people 'round there got to go to school, but I didn't. I went through the eighth grade, but I wasn't there most of the time.

Come Christmas time, us kids would take a shoe box we had and go around to people's houses on the first day of Christmas and say, "Good mornin', Christmas gift." They'd give us a candy or raisins—you know, them raisins on a stem—or an apple or orange. We'd go around to all the neighbor houses.

That was fun! We didn't buy no gifts, didn't give no didn't nobody give no gifts. No, we didn't know what that was. Wasn't no wrappin' nothin'. What you got, you got in that shoebox. We didn't get nothin' on Christmas day.

To make a little extra money through the year, we took in people's washin' and ironin'. We had wash bowls and tubs and pots that you boiled the clothes in. We put 'em in there and boiled 'em and then put 'em on a block and beat 'em with a stick. I never did know what that done. I guess we was beatin' the dirt out of 'em.

We slep' on what you called a hay mattress. We got hay from the fields and stuffed it inside them mattresses. When the mattress went flat, you opened it up, emptied out the hay, washed the mattress real good, and stuffed some new hay in there. Ever' time you rolled over on that mattress, you'd get stuck by a big piece of hay comin' through it.

We didn't have no 'tricity. We had coals. We'd work hard in the field in the daytime, iron at night by lamp, then go to sleep on them hay mattresses. It was hard. I come up the hard way.

LEE

On Finding a Kindred Spirit

From the very beginning there was a strong bond between Annie and me. I was inexplicably drawn to her. I remember being fascinated just watching her mouth move as she talked or her hands as she cooked. I loved listening to her tell stories of her childhood in the country and seeing the cotton fields, garden, and farmhouse come to life as she talked. Over and over again, I had her tell me the stories. Each time I would hear something different, understand something new.

There was no shortage of testosterone in our house. Growing up with three brothers was a challenge for me. I tried so hard to be big and play the tough games they played, but I never really made the grade. After each disappointment I took refuge in Annie's company. With one look, she knew. "I can tell you been playin' wit those boys again. You member what ol' Annie tole you, they wouldn't be pickin' on you if they didn't love you."

"But Annie, how do you know?" I asked.

"I jus' knows," she replied softly.

My memories of the early years are very sketchy. The routine trips to the grocery store with Mother, Daddy sitting at his desk balancing the checkbook, they seem to pale in significance to the special memories of a trip to the beach or a big snowstorm.

As I look back on it, everyone was busy, busy doing the things they were supposed to be doing. Daddy worked at the brokerage firm, handled the finances of the family, and took care of the yard and house, while Mother drove us where we needed to go, got involved with volunteer groups, and spent time with her friends. My brothers were in school, playing sports, and being boys. That left me, the baby, trying to squeeze myself into a full plate.

Even though Annie had her hands full with the housework and cooking, she made time for me. Naturally, I gravitated right to her. It is no wonder we became so close.

ANNIE

On Coming to Louisville

I got married when I was 17 years old. I met Oliver Patterson at the church. We run away and got married. You heard people talkin' 'bout elopin'? That's what I did. My family, my grandmother 'specially, didn't want me to get married. Wouldn't even let me have a boyfriend, hardly. They jus' needed me to work.

We was married by the Justice of the Peace. My uncle, who knew how my grandmother was and wanted to help me get away, he carried me to meet the man. My cousin went with me. I was jus' runnin' from so much work, but I been workin' ever since.

After we got married, we lived on a small cotton farm near my family. My daughter Hattie Del was born, near as I can think, when I was 18. Henry Lee was born two years later. And there was two years different with Addie Mae, my baby.

In 1937, Oliver got a call from his brother in Louisville, who tole him there was jobs up here. Oliver, he come up here and got hisself a job at Tube Turns —you know, over there at Broadway where they got all that iron—Broadway and 28th. After Oliver got his job and moved, he sent for me.

I come to Louisville and left the babies home. Henry Lee and Hattie Del stayed with their grandmother Hattie, Oliver's mama. Then about two months later, Hattie Del and Henry Lee come to Louisville. They come by theyselves. Oliver's mama tagged 'em and put 'em on the train. My mama kept Addie Mae, 'causin' she was still jus' a baby. Mama sent Addie on up to us later.

It was right after Louisville's Great Flood of 1937 when I moved here. Most all the water was gone by then—folks'd been rowin' boats through the downtown streets when the river was up—but you could still see all the mess and the damage to the storefronts.

I hadn't ever seen a real downtown before I come to Louisville. I liked the big department stores, like Stewart's on Fourth Street. Never did see nothin' like that in West Point, Georgia. But I come to find out when I tried on a hat in the department stores that I had to buy it if I tried it on—all 'causin' I was black, or "colored" as they said in them days. Never had nothin' like that happen down home, but only when I come to the big city.

People ast me did I have trouble findin' good housin' in Louisville in them days, bein' black and all. Only trouble we had was findin' a place that took children. Finally we found one, in the basement of a roomin' house. We rented out of Mr. Adam's house on Greenwood Avenue.

I was workin' for a woman named Mrs. Davis across't the street. I worked for her, let me see, two years—worked for her and her daughter both. Her daughter lived in back and had one daughter of her own. I did housework and helped out.

After that I worked at Kentucky Laundry. I cuffed and collared the shirts. I was a presser. I just did the cuffs and collars and passed the shirts on to someone else.

Then I was the head cook at Reynolds Metals', Plant 11, over in Portland. I worked there about three years, cooked for 300 people. I had to be to work at seven o'clock. Miz Solomon was my boss lady. I'd cook my meat day before so alls I had to do was slice it next morning, make my pies, and put dinner on the steam table. I'd make 25 to 30 pies ever' day. I had two ovens there, and they'd hold eight pies at a time. While my pies was cookin', I'd slice my meat.

I had some other girls helpin' me. They'd fix up the salad and the steam table. We had to have the food on the table at eleven o'clock. When them workers come in there to the cafeteria and seen all that food and them pies, they had a fit! Ate up every bit of it. Then we'd clean up and get ready for the next day. I was out of there 'bout three o'clock ever' day. But then they moved Plant 11 into Plant 9, and I was out of a job.

Soon enough I went to work at Lucky Strike cigarettes. I was feedin' tobacca through the machine. It was just a long, straight machine, all the way across't the factory floor. See, when the tobacca is hangin' up to dry in the bundle, it's tied in a knot. So they'd drop it on the machine, and when it come to me, the head of the bundle would done come off. All I did was spread the tobacca out where it go under the machine. On the end, there was a girl catchin' the stems—stemmin' it—and throwin' the stems in a box.

Right about then Oliver died, so we rented rooms from Miz Taylor. She was livin' by herself 'causin' her husband and son had passed. She was as sweet as she could be. She used to help me with my children, and I did a lot of her cookin'. Stayed with Miz Taylor 20 years. Unh hunh. She didn't want me to leave.

One of Miz Taylor's church members was workin' next door to a Miz Lanier, and she needed someone to help out wit' her baby. I wasn't workin' at Lucky Strikes no more, so I went to work for Miz Lanier. Then I come to find out about one of Miz Lanier's friends—Miz Rankin—and that she really needed me, too.

LEE

On Picking Poke and Other Wonders

It wasn't long after Annie came to work for us that we moved into a bigger house. Some of my earliest memories are of following Annie from room to room in that house.

When Annie was in the kitchen, I was right there watching everything she did. When she did the laundry, I followed her to the basement and watched and waited patiently. I remember watching her methodical movements as she ironed—back and forth, back and forth. I would stand there for what seemed like hours, probably hypnotized, watching her work that iron.

"Girl, go play wit' yo' toys!" Annie would command, exasperated. I would just shake my head and keep my eyes on the iron.

When the last of my older brothers was old enough for school, I had Annie to myself in the daytime. Our house had a large backyard, and there were woods and creeks and all sorts of fun places to play nearby. Annie and I would go for walks in the morning, down to the garden or into the woods.

"See this plant here," Annie said, pointing to a tall, leafy plant. "That's poke. You can tell it 'causin' it looks like tobacca and has this here red stem."

Annie bent the poke plant closer to me. "You can eat it while it's young, cook it up wit' greens. Once't it get berries though, it ain't no count—it's poison."

She plucked a reddish-purple berry from another poke plant and squeezed it into a Kleenex. "You don't want to get none of this on you, 'causin' it stain somethin' awful. Used to be, folks used 'em to dye they clothes."

I was all eyes and ears as Annie held forth with her plant folklore. These nature hikes and poke-picking expeditions continued throughout my childhood, and I always looked forward to the days when Annie was "fixin' greens."

ANNIE

On Love and Marriage

I 'member I was workin' for the Laniers, and Miz Lanier done tole me 'bout how all four of them Rankin kids had the chicken pops. Unh hunh. She said Miz Rankin was sick wit' the chicken pops too, and needed help takin' care of the children. So I came and looked after all of 'em.

Them Rankin kids was some tough little rats. By the end of the day, I'd be

 so tired when I got on the bus, I'd fall asleep and ride past my house.

For about three years I was workin' a few days at both the Rankins and the Laniers. But finally it come down to who needed me worst. That was a hard choice I had to make.

Miz Rankin, she needed me somethin' awful. That, and I loved my little Lee from the start. She was my white baby.

'Fore long, my mama took sick down in Georgia. I went down there and stayed with her for two months to wait on her. Miz Rankin called me and wrote me to come back. Yeah, she had a fit—but I had to go to Georgia, I had no choice. Miz Rankin, she done the best she could while I was gone, but that house was somethin' else when I got back.

See, I had to get back to the Rankins, and I wanted Mama to come back here where I could see about her. But she didn't want to come to Louisville. It was my pastor, Reverend C.C. Cloud, that talked her into a notion of comin' back with me. And that's the onliest reason she come. I got a man down there in Georgia with a ambulance, and he brought us back.

Mama got up here and got her a doctor, Dr. Milton Young. I think he's still in doctorin'. She didn't want nobody but him, 'causin' she was crazy 'bout Dr. Young. He helped her lots.

My children helped me take care of Mama. Addie and Hattie was grown and on they own, but they came and helped. Wasn't nobody with me but Henry Lee, and he worked at nights and watched Mama in the day. He'd be home 'til I got home, and, see, when I got home he'd go to bed 'til time to go to work. It worked out fine.

Henry Lee was so devoted to my mama. Addie and Hattie was too, 'causin' that was they heart—always tryin' to help those in need. I tried to raise up all'n my kids thataway. Henry Lee married soon after Mama passed. All my children stayed home 'til they got married. That's the way we done it back then.

One night a friend carried me to a party over to the church. My friends started talkin' 'bout me not havin' a man friend. One of my friends said she knew of a nice man named Jack Johnson. She tole him to call me, and he did. Jack come to see me the first day of January in 1980. And we got together— went together for a year. So really it was both a friend and the church that made us acquainted.

When Jack asked me to marry him, I was surprised. My feelin' was that Jack was a good man, but I didn't want to take no chances. So I called Miz Rankin 'causin' I needed some advice. She tole me I better know what I was doin'. She said she didn't want no man takin' advantage of Annie.

Miz Rankin didn't tell me 'til after, but she went to Stock Yards Bank, where Jack used to work. She knowed those men at the bank and she asked 'em about Jack. Know what they tole her? They tole her Jack was a fine person, and that Annie couldn't marry a better man. Later, she tole Jack what she done. Tole him, "You better be glad you a good man, Jack!" That was Miz

Rankin, didn't think nothin' 'bout goin' way outta her way when she really cared 'bout someone.

Jack and I got married on the 29th of November in 1980. All the Rankins was at the wedding. It was so beautiful. After we married, I left Greater Tabernacle Church and started goin' to Community Baptist Church 'causin' Jack was a deacon there. A family that prays together, stays together. Folks says that a lot, but it really is true.

Jack used to come when I served Christmas dinner at the Rankins' house. Said he wasn't gonna let me go off on Christmas Day without him. He washed all the dishes and the pots and pans. Wore his light blue coat and his white apron, and he looked just as handsome as could be. And when they had a party he'd come and help. Miz Rankin come and get us from the kitchen and some-body'd get up to the piano and play. Me and Jack, we'd stand right up there and sing Amazing Grace. Everybody loved it. Them was some days!

LEE

The Beginning of My Baking Career

When I was finally tall enough to reach the kitchen counter, Annie started letting me help her cook. She'd look down at me with a big smile and say, "We cookin' up a storm, girl!"

It was a special treat for both of us when I was home on the day Annie baked. She would announce early in the day, "I'm gonna get this dinner started, then I'll make a cake."

"Can I help you?" I would ask hopefully.

"Sure! You know Annie loves it when her baby helps her make a cake."

When I was seven, I started baking all by myself. That year, Santa brought me an Easy-Bake Oven. Powered by a 60-watt light bulb, it baked 4-inch round cakes and miniature cookies. Included with the little oven was an assortment of tiny boxes of baking mixes for chocolate and vanilla cakes, frostings, and cookies.

The day after Christmas, I turned the breakfast room table into my bakery. To the left of the Easy-Bake Oven was my mixing area, with little red plastic bowls, spoons, and cake pans. To the right was my cooling, icing, and display station. I was so excited when the small cakes and cookies came out of the oven. I iced the cakes the same way Annie iced hers. I was so proud, I ran through the house delivering my home-baked goodies to my brothers and parents.

By the end of the day, I had used up all the little boxes of mix. I went to bed heartbroken that my baking career was over nearly as soon as it had begun. The next morning at breakfast, I was quiet and sad.

Annie took one look at me and asked, "What's wrong wit' my baby? Cat got your tongue?"

"I ran out of my cake mix," I cried.

"Now, now, don't you worry your pretty little head. Let's see what ol' Annie can figures out."

She disappeared into the kitchen and came back with a big box of chocolate cake mix in her hand. "We'll use this. All we has to do is figure out how much for each cake."

While Annie cleaned up from breakfast, I set up my bakery again. We calculated the correct proportions: three spoons of cake mix to one spoon of water. Then I was off and baking again, grateful to Annie for solving what had seemed to me an impossible problem.

ANNIE
On Money

Now, Mr. Rankin—he's my buddy. He's been nice to me since the very first day I started to work for him and his family. After a while I come to him for help gettin' my savin's in order. I figure, that's what he do for a living—helps folks make money, and helps 'em keeps it once't they got it. Mr. Rankin, he helped me with my house—gave me a start. He done learn't me lots about business and how to handle money.

You know, some people just do it for you—whatever it is, they figure it's quicker to just do it theyselves. But Mr. Rankin didn't do that. He showed me how to handle my savin's and investin's so I'd learn. He still helps me out, when I need it. I don't think there is nobody in the world like Mr. Rankin.

LEE
On the Ride to Annie's House

As I became more involved with school, I saw Annie less. Some nights Annie stayed to fix dinner or to watch us while Mother and Daddy were out. At the end of the evening, Daddy would drive Annie home. I would find a way to stay up or I'd pretend that I couldn't sleep so that I could go with Daddy to take Annie home.

In my nightgown, snug in the warmth and safety of the car while the world outside was dark and quiet, I watched out the window as we made our way through downtown Louisville.

"Mr. Rankin, can I ast you a question?" Annie would start.

"Of course, Annie," my father would respond.

Annie would proceed to ask questions about her money and her savings. Daddy answered her questions, explaining why things in the financial world worked the way they did. Annie listened attentively and continued asking questions. I listened also, saving my own questions for the drive home.

When we arrived at Annie's house, she would pat me on the shoulder as she got out of the car.

"You be a sweet girl now, you hear?" she'd say to me, tenderly.

"I will," I assured her.

"Good night, Annie…thank you so much!" Daddy would call out.

Then Annie would let herself into the house and stand in the doorway to wave goodbye as we pulled away.

ANNIE
On Friendship

Now, Miz Rankin was a wonderful person. Won't ever be another one like her. She was so sweet. Unh hunh. Me and her was so close. I did all I could for Miz Rankin because we was best friends. She was so good to me.

Those last few months, I had to do more for her 'causin' she kept getting sick. I'd come to work and she'd still be up in the bed. That right there tole me somethin' was wrong, 'causin' she was most always awake when I got there. I'd go up to wish her a good mornin', and she'd say, "Annie, could you help me this mornin'?"

And I did, I helped her get cleaned up and I got her dressed. Seemed like she got kinda confused sometimes. But she always stayed a good person, and I never minded helpin' her one little bit.

After all the children was grown, I didn't work but two or three days a week. I kept workin' 'til I retired. That was after Miz Rankin died. If Miz Rankin had of lived, I'd probably still be there. She was my buddy. Me and her, we was so close.

I 'member the last time I seen Miz Rankin. She was leavin' for the hospital, and she went to say goodbye to Jenny, her dog. Lord, did she love that dog! She said, "Goodbye, Jenny. Mama won't see you no more." That was so sad. I sho' do miss Miz Rankin.

LEE
On Loss and Recovery

High school was a difficult time for me. I struggled with schoolwork. I felt socially inadequate, and things at home seemed to be falling apart. Within a two-year period, all my brothers went away to school or college. Daddy was now running the brokerage firm and facing a very challenging time in its history. Mother was in a battle for her life with alcoholism.

Although I didn't see Annie much during this period, she continued to provide for our needs and feed us in the same dependable way. I think it was her stable presence that helped get us through that time, especially Mother. Annie was able to see right past the disease to Mother's spiritual side. She treated her with such love and care, never doubting that Mother was strong enough to get well. Annie also was able to comfort my fear and concern for Mother, saying, "Jus' you watch, your mama's gonna be alright. Your mama's strong, and God's gonna help her."

Annie was right. Mother entered treatment and began a successful recovery program. By the grace of God we all made it through. Annie and Mother were closer than ever before. By this time I was working and living on my own, so I would stop by the house for lunch. The hours raced past as Mother, Annie, and I sat around the kitchen table, talking and looking at cookbooks. Jack often caught us still at the table with the lunch dishes in the sink when he came for Annie in the afternoon.

Within a few years, Mother's physical health began to deteriorate. On her bad days, Annie called me to come over before she left, and I stayed with Mother until Daddy got home. In this way, we surrounded her with comfort and support during those final months.

As I struggled with the intense emotions brought on by my mother's passing, once again Annie was there to provide a soothing balm for my feelings, clarity for my thoughts.

"It brought such joy to your mama," Annie explained, "to have you close by at the end, knowin' how much you loved her, and how proud you was of her."

ANNIE
On Slowing Down

Jack had three children, and I had three. Sometime after we got married, one of his daughters passed. It was hard on him. I was just glad we was together, so I could help him get through it. So now there's only two of his children.

He had the sugar sickness, you know, that diabetes. That's what made him sick. After he lost his eyesight, he went down the hill from there. Me and the children took care of him, the last two years. He passed on January 10th, 1994. We was married 14 years. Jack was the sweetest man, and we was so happy together.

My rheumatoid arthritis pains me now and again. I can sit right here and tell it's rainin' outside just as good as lookin' out the window. My knee goes to hurtin' like someone hittin' it with a hammer. Then it come up in my shoulder. When it hits, I fix me up a tonic and have that. Bad as it is, I just thank God that I'm doin' as good as I am. Yes Lord, I thank God. Bad as it is, it could be worse.

Nowadays I enjoy my grandchildren and great-grandchildren—those from my own children and those from Jack's children. I jus' try to keep a-busy. Your mind don't do right when you alone too much. If I feel like it, I get up and cook. Whatever I feel like doin', I do it.

LEE

On the Annie Lee Bakery

During the spring of 1991, Annie became very ill with congestive heart failure. Her doctors said she was near death.

I went to visit her daily in the hospital and, later, at her home. It was a touching experience for us both—me taking care of Annie and cooking for her, just as she had done for me all those years ago. As a result, our relationship transformed into something deeper and more spiritual in nature.

Annie recovered but suffered a setback a few years later, spending over a week in the hospital. Again I kept close tabs on her, and I knew she was feeling better when she tole me on the phone that she had a batch of rolls in the oven. It wouldn't be long, she said, before she would be baking pies and cakes for other people again.

"Praise the Lord!" she said. "It makes me feel so good to do for others. I jus' thank God I'm still able."

Then Annie's voice took on a nostalgic tone. "You and me work good together, Lee. If you lived closer we could open us a business. The Annie Lee Bakery business. Wouldn't that be somethin'?"

Annie was referring to a project we had jointly fantasized about since I was a little girl. It began one day when we were making a yellow cake with caramel icing for my brother's birthday.

"When I grow up, let's open a bakery," I said as I put icing on the cake. "We'll call it the 'Annie Lee Bakery.'"

"The Annie Lee Bakery! Wouldn't that be somethin'!" Annie exclaimed.

When we'd finished icing the cake, we stepped back to look at it. "Ain't that pretty!" Annie said. "Me and my baby's gonna open us a bakery. The Annie Lee Bakery."

Annie went back to the hospital again during the summer of 1996. This time it took a little longer before she was up and baking again. I asked her one day if she was planning to bake for the holidays. She was quiet for a while, and then she said, "I don't know, Lee. 'Cordin' to if the Lord lets me." I couldn't help myself as I wept softly at the thought of what it would mean to Annie if He didn't.

Sometime in October, I called Annie again and asked her if she was going to bake for Thanksgiving. "I ain't bakin' nothin' for nobody this year. I jus' can't do it no more." Her voice was flat.

"What if I came before Thanksgiving and helped you?" I asked cautiously.

"What you talkin' 'bout, girl?" Annie sounded much more animated now.

"If I came a couple of weeks early to help you," I repeated, "would you bake?"

"Yes! Oh Lord, yes! I jus' can't do it by myself no more." She was elated now. "My baby's comin' and helpin' her Annie cook for Thanksgiving. Praise the Lord!"

Excited at the prospect of cooking together again, we joked that we would finally open the Annie Lee Bakery. A friend designed a logo, and we had "Annie Lee Bakery" stickers printed. Early in November we called friends and family to tell them we were open for business.

The first day, we got together early for breakfast and made our master list of orders and compiled our grocery list. Then every day we began at seven and worked until noon. We started making rolls, but as soon as we were almost finished we'd get another order.

As we rolled out the very last roll, Annie said, "I don't wanna see another roll—ever. And when we pulls that last pan out the oven, I'm gonna dance on the table!" True to her word, she began to dance right then and there in front of the stove.

Next, we made pies and cakes. We baked and baked and baked until the smell of fresh dinner rolls and sweet pies wafted out to the sidewalk. Annie was having her whole family for Thanksgiving dinner, so we made that, too—huge roasting pans filled with macaroni and cheese, dressing, greens, and peach cobbler.

Everything was packaged in white boxes, stamped with the Annie Lee Bakery label, and tied with red string. We set up an area in the basement to warehouse all the finished orders. By the time we were finished, we'd made 60 dozen rolls, 25 pies, 2 cakes, and Thanksgiving dinner for 75—all the members of Annie's family.

On delivery day, Annie and I stood at the foot of the basement stairs and looked around. Every flat surface was covered with stacks of bakery boxes, and the whole room smelled of pumpkin pie.

Annie whistled. "I ain't never seen nothin' like this. Girl, we is in business!"

ANNIE
On the Goodness of the Lord

I try to make it day by day. I does the best I can and then I leave it up to God. My children, Jack's children, and our grandchildren and friends come to see 'bout me and they help me out. I don't know what I'd do without 'em.

You got to do right by others, and don't let nobody but God tell you who you are—that's between you and the Lord. Don't nobody else have the right to tell you.

I never in a million years dreamed that no one would ever make a book about me or my recipes. That's my Lee. I'll always be her Annie, and I'll always be there for her. That's why the Lord put us here on Earth—to love one another and do what we can for 'em.

The Lord is so good to me. I thank God for what I have. I come up the hard way, and now look at what all I done. Things don't always come when you want 'em, but they're on time.

Psalm 23

The Lord is my shepherd; I shall not want.

*He maketh me to lie down in the green pastures; He leadeth me
beside the still waters.*

*He restoreth my soul; He leadeth me in the paths of
righteousness for His name's sake.*

*Yea, though I walk through the valley of the shadow of death, I will fear
no evil; for Thou art with me; Thy rod and Thy staff they comfort me.*

*Thou preparest a table before me in the presence of mine enemies;
Thou anointest my head with oil; my cup runneth over.*

*Surely goodness and mercy shall follow me all the days of my life;
and I will dwell in the house of the Lord forever.*

Annie's Recipes

COOKIN' UP THE RECIPES

Annie Johnson's cooking has a certain style that is elegant in its simplicity. All of her recipe ingredients are whole—for example, a whole onion or a whole carrot, not two tablespoons of chopped onions or three tablespoons of diced carrots. If a recipe calls for egg yolk, the egg white is used in the same recipe. The simplicity of many of the recipes reflect Annie's early years living in the rural South, when dinner was put on the stove in the morning or early afternoon and left to cook while she went to work in the fields. It was a time when, out of necessity, people cooked with whatever they had at hand and nothing was wasted.

Annie has guarded her recipes quite jealously over the years, and rarely has she given them to anyone. Sitting with her at her kitchen table one morning, I gathered my courage and told her about my idea for this book. I was rather stunned when she answered enthusiastically and without hesitation, "Yes! Unh hunh! I like that idea!" Over several cups of coffee, we chatted about what recipes to include in the book. Each recipe reminded us of another, and then another. By the end of the morning, we had our list.

Most of her recipes exist only in Annie's head, and she has repeated them so many times there has been little need for a written copy. Annie likes to explain it this way: "You 'member when Mrs. Rankin asked me for my recipes and I told her, 'You gonna have to take me down to Mr. Rankin's office and put my head to that Xerox machine to get 'em.'" When she cooks, Annie just combines the ingredients, knowing by instinct and experience how much of everything to put in. As she says, "I don't follow a recipe really, 'causin' I know it." Annie's cozy kitchen is the heart of her house, which is situated in a quiet and well-tended section of Louisville. An old wooden china cabinet full of beautiful dishes is the focal point of the kitchen. Bright, patterned curtains frame the windows that overlook her deck and back yard. In the center of the room, a large oval table has a lazy Susan as its centerpiece. The kitchen cabinet holds four or five cookbooks, mostly from local churches and clubs. A few of Annie's hand-written recipes are held there between the pages, in no particular order.

As we talked about the promises and possibilities of this book, Annie peered at each of her scribbled recipes and recited the instructions. "But," she would add each time, looking up at me with a sly smile, "I don't do it that way."

I knew then that the recipe testing process would pose a great many challenges, and chief among them was the task of observing and interpreting Annie's actions in the kitchen and converting them to written instructions that—when carefully followed—would yield her phenomenal results for virtually anyone. Thanks to Annie's patience and expert guidance, I believe I have succeeded in this goal. The proof, as they say, is in the pudding—or in this case, it's in the pumpkin pie.

Annie spent her entire life gathering her recipes from family, friends, employers, and colleagues. Some recipes she created completely on her own. But on the occasions when I ask her about the origin of a specific recipe, Annie's stock answers include, "Lord, I been cookin' that dish since 'fore you was born," and "My remembers is gone."

To write the recipes for this book, Annie cooked while I took careful notes and asked questions. With a scale, I weighed the "handfuls" of this and "spoonfuls" of that. Later, when converting the weights into cups and tablespoons, I was amazed to find they were all even measurements. Annie's instinctive methods of measurement were so precise that they yielded no fractions to round off.

Annie is very much a morning person. Her personal philosophy has always been, "Early to bed and early to rise." During my visits to Louisville, Annie and I spent our mornings cooking and testing recipes together. I would land on her doorstep, usually before seven, with sacks of groceries in tow. Over breakfast, we'd discuss our game plan for the day. In Annie's words, "The earlier we get started, the earlier we get through. Ain't no need of stayin' in the kitchen all day."

There is very little counter space in her kitchen, so it is fortunate that Annie is a very well-organized cook. She starts each recipe with the sink empty, so it can be used for measuring and sifting dry ingredients; this procedure helps avoid making a mess. Annie has a board that she puts across the sink to roll out dough. At the end, she stops to clean up the kitchen. "Now, see how easy it is," Annie chides, "to clean as you go. I can't stand to have things dirty in the kitchen. Jus' ain't no way to do it."

Sometimes Annie would cook, showing me how she does it; other times she would tell me what to do, then sit down and watch. We worked well together throughout the recipe testing process, trading off tasks and helping each other out, all the while sharing stories from the past and laughing. One day she looked up from the meringue she was making and said, "I could just go on and on like this, every day. I am enjoyin' this!"

By midmorning, most of our cooking was finished. Annie would look at the clock and remark, "We got a lot done and it ain't twelve o'clock yet." The rest of the morning we spent packing up the food to give away, planning for the next day, and fixing our lunch. As word got out that we were cooking, friends and family began making well-timed drop-in visits, claiming they were "just in the neighborhood." We put them to work as taste testers and sent them home with a delicious plate of food.

Bread &
Breakfast

Bread and Breakfast

Bread

Banana Bread
Buttermilk Biscuits
Dinner Rolls
Salt Rising Bread
Hot Water Cornbread
Spoonbread
Yellow Cornbread

Breakfast

Buttermilk Pancakes
Cinnamon Rolls
Coffee Cake
Corn Cakes
French Toast
Fried Apples
Grits

When I first started to work for Miz Rankin, she asked me to make some rolls. Never made none in my life. I didn't have no recipe. But one came in my head. I was crazy enough to go in there and try to make 'em. They was the hardest things I ever ate. I thow'd 'em out in the yard, and the dog wouldn't eat 'em. Them rolls laid out there and the birds wouldn't eat 'em, neither.

She asked me to try again. So I just kept on 'til I got it together. I was so tickled when I did. So was Miz Rankin. After that, when I was making rolls, Miz Rankin used to come in the kitchen and eat some of the dough. She didn't want to lick the bowl, she ate the dough.

BANANA BREAD

YIELD: 1 LOAF
          350° OVEN

The Lord don't always come when you call, but He's always on time.

Ingredients:
1/2 **cup unsalted butter, softened**
1 **cup sugar**
2 **eggs**
3 **ripe bananas, mashed**
1 **teaspoon vanilla extract**
2 **cups all-purpose flour**
1 **teaspoon baking soda**
1/2 **teaspoon salt**
1 **cup chopped pecans or walnuts** (optional)

Method:
• Grease and flour a 5x9-inch loaf pan.
• Cream the butter and sugar together until light and fluffy.
• Add the eggs, one at a time, mixing well after each.
• Add the mashed bananas and vanilla extract. Mix to combine.
• Sift the flour, baking soda, and salt together. Add to the batter. Mix until just combined, being careful not to over mix.
• Add the nuts to the mixture and stir by hand to combine.
• Pour into the prepared loaf pan.
• Bake in a 350° oven for 1 hour, or until a toothpick inserted in the center comes out clean.

Note: Overmixing the batter after the flour is added will develop the gluten in the flour and make the bread tough.

BUTTERMILK BISCUITS

"When I first made biscuits I was out in the country, and we had lard. I ain't made no biscuits in a long time. I ain't made none since I was out to the Rankin's house. Used to have 'em ever' time we had hash."

YIELD: ONE DOZEN BISCUITS
400° OVEN

You can't jus' up and quit 'causin' somethin' is all messed up. You got to stay and help straighten it out.

Ingredients:
2 **cups all-purpose flour**
1 **tablespoon baking powder**
1/2 **teaspoon baking soda**
1 **teaspoon salt**
1/2 **cup solid vegetable shortening**
1 **cup buttermilk**
Additional flour for rolling out biscuits

Method:
· Sift the flour, baking powder, baking soda, and salt together into a medium-sized bowl. Cut the shortening into the flour.
· Add the buttermilk to the flour and work together with a spoon or by hand.
· Turn out onto a floured board. Using as much flour as you need, work the dough into a round disk. Roll out until the dough is 1/2 inch thick.
· Cut the biscuits, using a floured 2 1/2-inch round cutter. Gather the scraps of dough into a ball, roll out and cut again. Place the biscuits 2 inches apart on a baking sheet.
· Bake in a 400° oven for 20 minutes, or until the biscuits are golden brown.

Note: Annie takes the last few scraps of dough and hand forms them into one big biscuit. She calls this the "mammy" biscuit, and it's always the best of the bunch.

Dinner Rolls

"These won't be no trouble when you get used to it. This is easy. I wait 'til I get 'em all rolled out, then I bake the first pan I rolled out. For God's sake, let 'em be cold 'fore you roll 'em. You can let 'em rise in the 'frigerator or put 'em in there for a while. That way they won't be hard to roll out."

"After you cut the roll, fold it even and kinda mash it down so it won't pop open. And don't use but one hand in the butter, then you only have one hand messed up."

Yield: 4 dozen rolls
400° oven

It's a blessin' to give to other people.

Ingredients:
1/2 **cup unsalted butter**
1/4 **cup solid vegetable shortening**
1 **cup milk**
1/2 **cup sugar** (divided into two)
2 **packages** (1/4 **ounce each**) **active dry yeast** (fast rising)
1 **cup warm water** (100°–120°)
1 **egg, well beaten**
5 **cups all-purpose flour**
1 **tablespoon salt**
1/2 **cup unsalted butter, melted**
Additional flour for rolling out dough

Method for dough:
• In a 6-quart pot, melt 1/2 cup butter and the vegetable shortening with the milk.
• Mix in half of the sugar (1/4 cup) and set aside to cool.
• In a small bowl, mix the remaining sugar (1/4 cup) with the yeast. Add the warm water, stirring to combine.

- Add the egg and the yeast mixture to the melted butter and milk. Stir gently.
- Sift the flour and salt together. Add half of the flour to the mixture and work together with a spoon or by hand. Add the rest of the flour and combine well.
- Cover loosely with a towel, lid, or plate and place in a warm place to rise for 1 1/2—2 hours. The mixture will double in size.
- Place in the refrigerator for 1/2 hour to make the dough easier to roll out.

Note: To activate the yeast, the water needs to be between 100°–120°. If it is too hot, it can kill the yeast. Since our body temperature is 98.6°, the water will feel warm but not hot when it is at the right temperature.

Method for rolling dough:
- Lightly grease 4 8x8x2-inch pans.
- Melt 1/2 cup of butter.
- Working in small batches, place a section of the dough on a well-floured board and work into a ball, using enough flour to keep it from sticking.
- Flour the board again and roll the dough to a thickness of 1/8 inch.
- Using a biscuit cutter, cut the dough into 2 1/2-inch rounds.
- With your hand or a pastry brush, pat both sides of each dough circle with melted butter, fold in half, and press lightly around the edges.
- Place in baking pans, spacing the rolls so that they barely touch and have room to rise (3 rolls across and 4 rolls up and down).
- Keep rolling out the dough. Place each filled pan in a warm place to rise for about 30 minutes or until doubled in size.
- Bake in a 400° oven until golden brown, about 18 minutes.
- Brush the tops with melted butter as soon as the pans come out of the oven.
- Serve warm with butter.

Note: Annie is famous for these rolls. They were served at special dinners and cocktail parties in the Rankin household and Annie often made them in large quantities for dinners at her church as well as ours. For years they were served at the annual Scholarship Luncheon at St. Marks Episcopal Church and listed on the menu as "Annie's Rolls."

SALT RISING BREAD

YIELD: 2 LOAVES
350° OVEN

If you let the Lord lead,
you don't got to push,
you jus' follow.

Ingredients:
2 **medium potatoes**
3 **tablespoons white cornmeal**
3 **tablespoons sugar**
2 **teaspoons plus 1 tablespoon salt**
3 **cups boiling water**
1 **cup milk**
2 **tablespoons solid vegetable shortening**
2 **teaspoons baking powder**
1 **teaspoon baking soda**
8 **cups all-purpose flour** (divided into two)
1/4 **cup unsalted butter**

Method:
Day One (preferably around noon):
• Peel and coarsely grate the potatoes.
• Put the potatoes, cornmeal, sugar, and 2 teaspoons of salt in a 1 quart glass jar or pitcher, or other non-reactive container.
• Pour boiling water over the potato mixture; stir and cover loosely.
• Keep in a warm place overnight. (see note next page)

Day Two (morning):

The potato liquid should have 1/2 inch or more of gray or light brown foam on top with a very distinctive odor!

- Grease two 5x9-inch loaf pans.
- Strain the potato mixture. Reserve the liquid and discard the potatoes.
- Bring the milk to a simmer and add the shortening to melt.
- Remove from the heat and stir in the baking powder, baking soda, potato liquid, and 1 tablespoon of salt.
- With a spoon, stir in 4 cups of the flour to make a thick batter, and leave to rise in a warm place until double in size (1 1/2-2 hours).
- Work in the remaining 4 cups of flour to make a stiff dough.
- On a floured surface, knead the dough for about 10 minutes or until it becomes smooth and elastic. Shape into 2 loaves and place in greased loaf pans.
- Bake in a 350° oven for 1 hour, or until the loaves are golden brown on top.
- Melt butter and brush the tops of the loaves after the bread has been in the oven for 50 minutes. Brush the tops with more butter when you bring them out of the oven.

Note: This is a two-day project. On Day One, you make a fermented liquid mixture, and on Day Two, you use the liquid to make the bread. The mixture needs a warm place for fermentation to happen. When Annie makes this she sits the mixture over the heat vent. I warm my oven (on the lowest setting for just a few minutes) and place the mixture inside with a pan of hot water. I then repeat the process a couple of times, keeping the mixture out of the oven until it is warm and turned off.

You got to do right by others and don't let nobody but God tell you who you are. That's between you and the Lord. Don't nobody else have no right to tell you.

HOT WATER CORNBREAD

YIELD: 7–10 PATTIES

Ingredients:
2 cups white cornmeal
2 teaspoons baking soda
1 teaspoon salt
2 tablespoons bacon grease, lard, or solid vegetable shortening
2 cups boiling water
Oil or vegetable shortening for frying

Method:
• Mix the corn meal, baking soda, and salt together in a medium-sized bowl.
• Add the bacon grease, lard, or shortening. Using your hands or a pastry blender, combine with the cornmeal.
• Add boiling water slowly, stirring well with a spoon until the cornmeal comes together into a ball.
• Run some cold water over your hands to keep the mixture from sticking, and mold into patties 1/2 inch thick and 3 inches in diameter.
• Heat 1/4 inch deep of oil or shortening in a skillet. Fry the patties about 2 minutes on each side until they are golden brown.
• Split the patties in half, and serve with butter while still hot.

Note: Bacon grease or lard gives the best flavor.

SPOONBREAD

YIELD: 8 SERVINGS
375° OVEN

Ingredients:
6 **eggs, separated**
4 **cups milk**
1 **cup white cornmeal**
2 **teaspoons salt**
1 **teaspoon baking powder**
4 **tablespoons unsalted butter**

Method:
- Before turning on the oven, space the racks so that there is room for the spoonbread to rise.
- Butter a 2-quart casserole (with high sides) or soufflé dish.
- Beat the egg whites until they are stiff.
- Beat the egg yolks in small bowl.
- In a medium-sized pot, heat the milk to a simmer and add the cornmeal slowly, stirring constantly. Continue to stir and cook over medium heat until thick.
- Remove from heat and add the salt, baking powder, butter, and egg yolks. Beat vigorously to combine.
- Fold in the beaten egg whites and pour into the buttered casserole dish.
- Bake in a 375° oven for 45 minutes. Turn the oven up to 400° for the last 5 minutes to brown the top.

Serve at the table in the casserole dish with a large spoon and have butter available.

This dish comes out of the oven looking like a soufflé, and it tastes so good. Spectacular!

YELLOW CORNBREAD

Food's ready. Don't need

nothin' but eatin'

Ingredients:
1/2 **cup butter, melted**
1 **cup buttermilk, room temperature**
2 **eggs, well beaten**
1 **cup yellow cornmeal**
1 **cup flour**
1 **teaspoon baking powder**
1 **teaspoon salt**
1 **tablespoon sugar** (optional)

Method:
• Preheat oven to 425°
• Generously grease an 8-inch cast iron skillet or
  8-inch square pan and place in the oven to heat.
  (The pan should be hot when the cornmeal mixture is
  poured into it.)
• Combine melted butter and buttermilk and stir in the
  well-beaten eggs.
• In a medium-sized mixing bowl, combine the cornmeal,
  flour, baking powder, and salt and mix well.
• Stir the buttermilk mixture into the cornmeal and mix
  until just incorporated. The batter may be a little lumpy.
  Do not overmix.
• Pour the batter into the heated pan.
• Bake in the middle of the oven at 425° for 20 minutes,
  or until the top of the bread is golden brown.

BUTTERMILK PANCAKES

YIELD: 16 PANCAKES

Ingredients:
2 **eggs**
2 **cups buttermilk**
2 1/4 **cups all-purpose flour**
1 **tablespoon sugar**
1 **teaspoon salt**
1 **teaspoon baking soda**
Vegetable oil

Method:

- Beat the eggs well in a medium-sized bowl. Add the buttermilk and mix well.
- Sift the flour, sugar, salt, and baking soda together and add to liquid mixture. Stir until well blended, but do not overmix.
- Heat a griddle or skillet with some vegetable oil. When medium hot, pour 1/4 cup of the batter for each cake.
- Turn the pancakes when bubbles form on the surface and the edges turn brown. Cook on the other side for one minute, or until the pancakes are golden brown.
- Serve with butter and warm maple syrup.

CINNAMON ROLLS

YIELD: 5 DOZEN ROLLS
400° OVEN

*When you live right,
don't nothin' slip
up on you.*

Ingredients for dough:
1/2 **cup unsalted butter**
1/4 **cup solid vegetable shortening**
1 **cup milk**
1/2 **cup sugar** (divided into two)
2 **packages** (1/4 **ounce each**) **active dry yeast**
  (not fast rising)
1 **cup warm water** (100°-120°)
1 **egg, well beaten**
5 **cups all-purpose flour**
1 **tablespoon salt**
Additional flour for rolling out dough

Ingredients for filling:
1 **cup unsalted butter, melted**
1 **cup white sugar**
1 **cup brown sugar**
2 **tablespoons ground cinnamon**

Method for dough:
• Melt the butter and vegetable shortening with the milk
  in a 6-quart pot.
• Mix in half the sugar (1/4 cup) and set aside to cool.
• In a small bowl, mix the remaining sugar (1/4 cup) with
  the yeast. Add the warm water and stir to combine.
• Add the egg and the yeast mixture to the butter and
  milk. Stir gently.
• Sift the flour and salt together.
• Add half the flour and work into the mixture with a
  spoon or by hand.

- Add the rest of the flour and combine well. Cover loosely with a towel, lid, or plate and place in warm place to rise for 1 1/2-2 hours. The mixture will double in size.
- Place in the refrigerator for 1/2 hour; this will make the dough easier to roll out.

Note: To activate the yeast, the water needs to be between 100°–120°. If it is too hot, it can kill the yeast. Since our body temperature is 98.6°, the water will feel warm but not hot when it is at the right temperature.

Method for filling:
- Melt 1 cup butter.
- Combine both the sugars and the ground cinnamon in a small mixing bowl.

Method for rolling the dough:
- Lightly grease four 8x8x2-inch pans.
- Working with 1/4 of the dough at a time, work the dough into a ball on a well-floured board. Keep remaining dough covered.
- Flour the board again and roll the dough to a thickness of 1/8 inch to form an 16x8-inch rectangle.
- Sprinkle 1/2 cup of cinnamon sugar over the dough, staying 1 inch away from the top edge and 1/2 inch away from the side edges.
- Drizzle 1/4 cup of melted butter over the sugar-covered dough, using just enough to wet the sugar.
- Roll up the dough from the bottom to the top and cut the roll into 1-inch slices.
- Place in a baking pans with the rolls barely touching (4 rolls across and 4 rolls down). Put aside in a warm place to rise for 1/2 hour.
- Keep rolling out remaining portions of dough.
- Bake in a 400° oven for 18 minutes, or until golden brown.

Note on sugar and butter: If you use too much melted butter in the filling, the mixture will flow out when you cut the rolls. If this happens, spoon it over the rolls when they are in the pan. Don't worry if there are "dry sugar" areas when you roll up the dough. The sugar melts during cooking.

Coffee Cake

"They call this a Sock-It-To-Me Cake. Lots of people make it from a cake mix, but I make it from scratch."

Yield: 1 bundt pan
350° oven

*People's always tellin'
me they don't see how
I do it, and I told 'em,
ain't nothin' but the
Lord. That's right. And
it's somethin' that keep
you pushin', you know,
don't let you give up.*

Ingredients:
8 eggs, separated
2 cups unsalted butter
2 cups white sugar
1 1/2 teaspoon vanilla extract
3 3/4 cups all-purpose flour
1 teaspoon salt
1/2 cup heavy cream
1 cup brown sugar
3/4 cup chopped pecans
1 tablespoon cinnamon
Powdered sugar

Method:
• Grease and flour a bundt pan.
• Beat the egg whites until they form soft peaks. Set aside.
• Cream the butter and sugar together.
• Add the egg yolks, a little at a time, mixing well after
  each addition.
• Add the vanilla extract.
• Sift the flour and salt together.
• Add the flour and cream alternately, starting and ending
  with flour. Mix well after each addition.

- Fold in the beaten egg whites.
- Pour half of the batter into the pan and smooth out the top.
- Mix together the brown sugar, pecans, and cinnamon. Sprinkle over the batter.
- Pour the second half of the batter into the pan and smooth out the top.
- Bake in a 350° oven for 1 1/2 hours, or until a tooth pick inserted in the center comes out clean.
- Cool for 10 minutes. If necessary, loosen the cake by running a knife around the edge of the pan. Turn the cake out onto a rack.
- Sprinkle with powdered sugar before serving.

Corn Cakes

Yield: 16 corn cakes

When you try and cook good, you always mess up. You got to jus' be yourself and cook.

Ingredients:
2 **eggs**
2 **cups buttermilk**
2 1/4 **cups all-purpose flour**
1 **tablespoon sugar**
1 **teaspoon salt**
1 **teaspoon baking soda**
1 **can (8 1/2 ounces) creamed corn**
Vegetable oil

Method:
• Beat the eggs well in a medium-sized bowl.
• Add the buttermilk, mixing well.
• Sift the flour, sugar, salt, and baking soda together and
  add to the liquid mixture.
• Add the creamed corn. Stir until well blended,
  but do not overmix.
• Heat a griddle or skillet with some vegetable oil.
  When medium hot, pour 1/4 cup of the batter for each
  corn cake.
• Turn the corn cakes when bubbles form on the surface
  and the edges turn brown. Cook on the other side for
  one minute, or until the corn cakes are golden brown.
• Serve with butter and warm maple syrup for breakfast
  or with turkey hash (see recipe page   ) for dinner.

French Toast

Yield: 10 slices

Ingredients:
6 **eggs**
1/2 **cup milk**
10 **slices of white bread**
Powdered sugar
Vegetable oil for cooking

Method:
- Heat a skillet or griddle with a thin coating of oil.
- Beat the eggs and milk together in a shallow container large enough to hold a flat slice of bread.
- When the skillet or griddle is hot, lay one piece of bread in the egg mixture and soak each side twice.
- Transfer the bread to the skillet and cook on each side until golden brown.
- Serve sprinkled with powdered sugar and/or maple syrup.

Variation:
Use cinnamon, French, or whole wheat bread for a different effect.

FRIED APPLES

"Ain't nothin' like fried apples with a big breakfast of grits, eggs, bacon, and biscuits."

YIELD: 6 SERVINGS

Your mind don't do right when you alone too much. That's why I keep a-busy. If I feel like it, I get up and cook. Whatever I feel like doin', I do it.

Ingredients:
6 **apples**
1/4 **cup unsalted butter**
1/3 **cup sugar**
2 **teaspoons cinnamon**

Method:
• Peel, core, and slice the apples into 1/4-inch wedges.
• Melt the butter in a skillet and fry the apples until they begin to soften.
• Combine the sugar and cinnamon in a small bowl, mixing well. Add to the apples and stir gently to combine.
• Cook until the apples become soft and translucent.

Note: If the apples are crisp, you can add a little water (2 tablespoons) to the skillet to help them cook.

GRITS

"Start with the grits in cool water and then add lots of butter. It makes 'em creamy."

YIELD: 6 SERVINGS

Ingredients:
4 **cups water**
1 **teaspoon salt**
1 **cup old-fashioned grits** (not quick-cooking)
1/4 **cup unsalted butter**

Method:
- Put the water, salt, and grits in a medium-sized pot on medium heat.
- Stir constantly until the water is steaming.
- Add butter, continuing to stir until the grits get thick and soft. (They will loose their "gritty" texture when cooked). It takes about 15 minutes from start to finish.

Note: Leftover grits can be poured into a square pan and spread out to a thickness of 1 inch. Cover and refrigerate overnight. The next morning, turn the grits out of the pan, cut them into any shape you like, and fry them until they're golden brown on both sides.

Soups, Sides, and Salads

Soups, Sides, and Salads

Soups
Navy Bean Soup
Split Pea Soup

Sides
Au Gratin Potatoes
Baked Beans
Black-Eyed Peas
Cheese Grits
Corn Pudding
Fried Green Tomatoes
Dressing
Green Beans
Greens
Macaroni and Cheese
Mashed Potatoes
Okra
Sweet Potato Casserole
Turnips

Salads, Spreads, and Snacks
Benedictine
Cheese Coins
Chicken Salad
Cole Slaw
Cooled Carrots
Potato Salad

Pickles
Bread-and-Butter Pickles
Chow Chow

Beverages
Fruit Punch
Spice Tea

When I was in the country, I had to get up every morning at four o'clock and cook five of them long pans of biscuits... and bacon, sausage, all that stuff. We raised all that back then. And when I run off and got married, I thought I wouldn't have to work. I been workin' hard ever since. And you know what I fed my new husband, Oliver, for breakfast that first mornin'? Jus' biscuits cooked on the top of the stove and some picnic bread and some ol' white back meat. That's all I had. I'd left all that country ham and chicken and all that stuff. Yeah, it was rough. You think you got it bad at home, and then when you run off, you want to run back.

NAVY BEAN SOUP

YIELD: 8 SERVINGS

I like to treat peoples as I want to be treated. That's the way I was taught, way I was brought up. I try to get along with people. That way you let somebody else know that you know God. Because if you know God, you need to spread that. If you live that way, certain people can see it and some people can't. But you don't worry about the ones that can't see it. Just keep a-livin'.

Ingredients:
1 **pound dried navy beans**
1 **ham hock**
2 **tablespoons oil**
1 **small onion, chopped small**
3 **carrots, chopped small** (optional)
1 **tablespoon salt**
1/2 **teaspoon pepper**

Method:
· Wash and soak beans overnight with three times as much water.
· In a small pot, cover the ham hock with water and boil for at least 1/2 hour.
· Heat the oil in a 6-quart soup pot and cook the chopped onion until soft.
· Drain the beans and add to the onions.
· Add the ham hock and its cooking water. Add the carrots (if using). Add water to cover, and salt and pepper.
· Simmer until the beans are tender (1 1/2-2 hours), adding water if needed.
· Using a potato masher, mash some of the beans in the pot. Thin the soup if necessary.
· Take the ham hock out of the soup. Remove all the skin and fat. Pull the meat off the bone and add it back into soup.
· Season with salt and pepper.

This one is a favorite of my father's, but he doesn't like carrots. Annie says, "I leaves the carrots out when I make it for Mr. Rankin."

SPLIT PEA SOUP

YIELD: 8 SERVINGS

Ingredients:
1 **ham hock**
2 **tablespoons oil**
1 **small onion, chopped small**
3 **celery stalks, chopped small**
3 **carrots, chopped small**
1 **pound green split peas**
2 **teaspoons salt**
1/2 **teaspoon pepper**

Method:
· Cook the ham hock with enough water to cover until tender, about 2 hours.
· In a 6-quart soup pot, heat the oil and cook the onion and celery until tender.
· Add the ham hock with its cooking water, the carrots, split peas, salt, and pepper.
· Add just enough water to cover. Simmer until split peas are tender, about 1 hour.
· Take the ham hock out of the soup. Remove all the skin and fat. Pull the meat off the bone and add it back into soup.
· Season with salt and pepper.

AU GRATIN POTATOES

YIELD: 8 SERVINGS
350° OVEN

There's people who talk about God all the time, but then they don't act like they really know Him. And then there's people who don't say nothin', but you can tell it by the way they live and the way they act that they know God.

Ingredients:
4 **medium potatoes**
4 **tablespoons unsalted butter**
2 **tablespoons all-purpose flour**
2 **cups milk**
2 **teaspoons salt**
1 **teaspoon white pepper**
8 **ounces (2 cups) cheddar cheese, grated**

Method:
• Butter a shallow 2-quart casserole dish.
• Peel and slice the potatoes into 1/4 inch circles, cover with cold water, and set aside.
• Melt the butter in a saucepan over low heat. Add the flour and stir until well combined. When the flour and butter are hot, gradually add the milk a little at a time, stirring well. Season with salt and pepper.
• Place half the potatoes in the casserole dish, add half the sauce and half the cheese. Make a second layer with the remaining ingredients.
• Bake in a 350° oven for 45 minutes, or until the potatoes are tender and the top is golden brown.

BAKED BEANS

Ingredients:
1 pound dried navy beans
1 small onion, chopped small
1 tablespoon salt
1/2 pound smoked salt pork or bacon, cut
  into 1-inch pieces
1/4 cup brown sugar
1 tablespoon Worcestershire sauce
1/4 cup molasses
Salt and pepper to season

Method:
• Wash and soak beans overnight with three times as
  much water.
• Drain the beans and add enough fresh cold water
  to cover.
• Add all the other ingredients, stirring to combine.
• Simmer covered until the beans are tender,
  about 1 1/2-2 hours.
• Season with salt and pepper.

BLACK-EYED PEAS

YIELD: 8 SERVINGS

Ingredients:
1 pound dried black-eyed peas
1 ham hock
1 teaspoon salt
1/4 teaspoon pepper

Method:
- Wash and soak peas overnight with three times as much water.
- Cook the ham hock in a large pot with enough water to cover for at least a 1/2 hour.
- Drain the beans and add them to the ham hock, adding enough fresh water to cover. Add salt and pepper.
- Simmer covered for about 1 1/2-2 hours, or until the beans are tender, stirring occasionally.
- Take the ham hock out of the pot. After removing all the skin, pull the meat off the bone and add this back into the bean pot.
- Season with salt and pepper.

CHEESE GRITS

YIELD: 8 SERVINGS
325° OVEN

Ingredients:
8 **cups water**
2 **cups old-fashioned grits**
2 **teaspoons salt**
1 **cup unsalted butter**
8 **ounces (1 1/2 cups plus 1/2 cup) cheddar cheese,
  grated**
4 **eggs, beaten**
2 **cups milk**

Method:
· Butter a 2-quart casserole dish.
· Put the water, grits, and salt in a 4-quart pot on
  medium heat. Stir constantly until water begins to
  show signs of being hot.
· Add the butter, continuing to stir. Keep stirring until
  the grits get thick and soft. (They will loose their
  "gritty" texture when cooked. It takes about 15 minutes
  from start to finish.)
· Add 1 1/2 cups of the cheese and stir until melted.
  Remove from the heat and add the eggs and the milk.
  Stir well.
· Pour the mixture into the casserole dish and sprinkle
  the top with the remaining 1/2 cup of cheese
· Bake in a 325° oven for 40 minutes, or until the top is
  golden brown.

CORN PUDDING

"Ever' body love this corn puddin'. I used to tell 'em there ain't nothin' to it — it's easy to make."

YIELD: 8 SERVINGS
350° OVEN

Oh, the Lord is so good. The Lord give you what you need.

Ingredients:
4 **eggs**
1 **cup cream**
1/4 **cup sugar**
1/2 **teaspoon salt**
1 **pound frozen corn, thawed**
4 **tablespoons unsalted butter**

Method:
· Butter a 2-quart casserole dish.
· In large bowl, beat the eggs, cream, sugar, and salt together. Add the corn and stir to combine.
· Pour the corn mixture into the buttered casserole dish.
· Slice the butter and arrange on top of the corn mixture.
· Bake in a 350° oven for 1 hour, or until the top is golden brown and the casserole is set.

FRIED GREEN TOMATOES

YIELD: 8 SERVINGS

Ingredients:
1/2 **cup white cornmeal**
1 **teaspoon salt**
1/2 **teaspoon black pepper**
4 **green tomatoes**
Oil for frying

Method:
- Heat a thin layer of oil in a skillet.
- Combine the cornmeal, salt, and pepper in a bowl or container wide enough to lay a slice of tomato flat.
- Core and slice the tomatoes. Coat in cornmeal mixture and fry on both sides until golden brown and tender.
- Drain on layers of paper towels.

Dressing

"Ever' body love this dressin'. I always make extra for the Rankins' holiday dinners, they eat so much of it. That's why this recipe makes a lot."

Yield: 12 servings
            350° oven

See, I think that is the reason people don't do no better, 'causin' they don't try. Gots to keep a-tryin'. Can't give up.

Ingredients:
4 **tablespoons vegetable oil or shortening**
1 **large onion, chopped small**
1 **green pepper, chopped small**
3 **celery stalks, chopped small**
2 **pounds dry bread cubes***
6 **eggs, well beaten**
3 **tablespoons dried sage**
2 **tablespoons salt** (omit unless using low salt stock)
2 **tablespoons poultry seasoning**
1 **teaspoon pepper**
1/2 **cup unsalted butter, melted**
4 **cups (two 17 3/4-ounce cans) turkey or chicken stock**

Method:
• Heat the oil in a skillet and cook the chopped onion, green pepper, and celery until tender.
• Combine the bread, eggs, and spices in a large bowl. Mix well.
• Pour the butter and stock in and stir well. Add water if necessary to make the dressing wet enough to mold into balls. There should be enough liquid that the bread cubes are soft.

- Mold the dressing into 2 1/2-inch balls and place in pans with 2-inch sides.
- Bake in a 350° oven for 40-45 minutes, or until they begin to turn golden brown and the inside is moist but not wet.

Note: For dry bread cubes, you can use packaged bread stuffing mix from the grocery store, or you can make your own. Cut or tear day old bread into pieces and lightly toast in a 250° oven for 15-20 minutes.

Variation for Cornbread Stuffing:
Replace 1 pound of dry bread cubes with crumbled yellow cornbread (see recipe page 38).

GREEN BEANS

YIELD: 8 SERVINGS

Ingredients:
1 ham hock or 1/4 pound salt pork, cut in
  1-inch pieces
2 pounds green beans
1/8 teaspoon baking soda
Salt and pepper

Method:
• Put the ham hock or salt pork in a 6-quart stock pot with enough water to cover. Cook until the meat is tender, about 2 hours.
• Remove stems and tips of beans. Break or cut into 2-inch pieces. Wash in cold water.
• Add the beans to the meat and cook uncovered until they are tender and very little water is left in the pot, about 1 hour.
• If you are using a ham hock, take it out of the pot and remove all the skin and fat. Pull the meat off the bone and add this back into the pot of beans.
• Season with salt and pepper.

GREENS

"I don't have enough strength to cut up them greens, so I jus' tear 'em up. I used to cut 'em up. I can't no more."

YIELD: 6 SERVINGS

Ingredients:
1 **ham hock or 1/4 pound salt pork, cut in 1-inch pieces**
3 **pounds greens (collard, mustard, kale, or a combination of the three, see note below)**
1/8 **teaspoon baking soda**
Salt and pepper

Method:
• Put the ham hock or salt pork in a 6-quart stock pot with enough water to cover. Cook until the meat is tender, about 2 hours.
• Remove the large stems from the greens and cut or tear into bite-sized pieces. Wash well in plenty of cold water.
• Add the greens to the meat and cook uncovered until they are tender and very little water is left in the pot, about 1 1/2 hours.
• If you are using a ham hock, take it out of the pot and remove all the skin and fat. Pull the meat off the bone and add this back into the pot of greens.
• Season with salt and pepper.

Note: There are many varieties of greens, and each has a distinctive flavor that will characterize the final taste of this dish. When deciding what to purchase, keep in mind that collard greens have a bland flavor, kale gives a cabbage flavor, while mustard greens make the dish taste of mustard.

MACARONI AND CHEESE

YIELD: 8 SERVINGS
350° OVEN

You know, when you can do somethin' to help somebody, it makes you feel glad. Yes, Lord!

Ingredients:
2 1/2 **tablespoons salt**
4 **cups uncooked macaroni (1 pound)**
1/4 **cup vegetable oil**
1/4 **cup all-purpose flour**
3 **cups milk**
1/2 **teaspoon salt**
1 **pound (3 cups plus 1 cup) sharp cheddar cheese, grated**

Method:
· Butter a 2-quart casserole dish.
· In a large pot, bring 6 quarts of water and 2 1/2 tablespoons of salt to a boil.
· Add the macaroni and cook until almost tender. It should still be a little chewy.
· Drain the macaroni and rinse with cold water. Pour into the buttered casserole dish and set aside.
· To make the sauce, heat the oil in a skillet and add the flour, stirring and cooking over medium heat until all the lumps are gone. Slowly add in the milk, stirring all the time. Bring to a boil and simmer for 10 minutes.
· Add 1/2 teaspoon of salt and 3 cups of the cheese to the sauce and stir until melted. Pour over the macaroni and stir to combine.
· Sprinkle the remaining 1 cup of cheese on top of the dish.
· Bake in a 350° oven for 30-40 minutes, or until the cheese topping is golden brown.

MASHED POTATOES

YIELD: 8 SERVINGS

Ingredients:
6 **medium baking potatoes**
1 **cup unsalted butter, melted**
1/2 **cup milk, warmed**
2 **teaspoons salt**
1/4 **teaspoon white pepper**

Method:
- Peel and quarter the potatoes. Add to boiling water. Adjust the heat, cover, and cook for about 20-30 minutes or until tender. Drain.
- Melt the butter and warm the milk.
- With a potato masher, mash the potatoes while pouring in the melted butter.
- Pour in warm milk, mashing and stirring until smooth.
- Season with salt and pepper.

OKRA

"Jack and I used to have a whole lot of okra in the garden out back. I'd pick it and freeze it so we'd have some all year round. Gotta pick it 'fore it get too big or it'll be tough and stringy."

YIELD: 8 SERVINGS

Ingredients:
2 pounds whole okra, fresh or frozen
4 tablespoons unsalted butter
1/2 cup water
2 teaspoons salt
1/4 teaspoon pepper

Method:
- Wash the okra, or thaw if frozen, and cut off the stems.
- Place the okra, butter, water, salt, and pepper in a pot and simmer, covered, until soft, about 40 minutes.

Sweet Potato Casserole

Yield: 8 servings
350° oven

Ingredients:
8 medium sweet potatoes
1/4 teaspoon nutmeg
1 teaspoon cinnamon
1/4 teaspoon salt
4 tablespoons unsalted butter
1/3 cup white sugar
1/3 cup brown sugar
1/2 cup chopped pecans
1 cup miniature marshmallows (optional)

Method:
- Butter a 2-quart casserole dish.
- Cut each sweet potato into eight pieces. Place in a medium-sized pot, cover with water, and boil until the potatoes are tender.
- Drain, peel, and mash the potatoes.
- Add the nutmeg, cinnamon, salt, butter, and both the sugars. Stir well.
- Place in the buttered casserole dish and sprinkle with chopped pecans and marshmallows (optional).
- Bake in a 350° oven for 30 minutes.

TURNIPS

YIELD: 8 SERVINGS

Yeah, that worryin' gets next to your nerves. Got to pray over it and jus' go on to sleep.

Ingredients:
2 pounds turnips
4 tablespoons unsalted butter
1 teaspoon salt
1/4 teaspoon pepper

Method:
· Peel and cut the turnips into 1 1/2-inch pieces.
· Place in a pot with just enough water to cover and add butter, salt, and pepper.
· Simmer covered until tender, about 30 minutes.
· Season with salt and pepper.

BENEDICTINE

YIELD: 1 1/2 POUNDS OF SANDWICH SPREAD

Ingredients:
1 pound cream cheese, softened
2 small cucumbers, seeded and grated (see note below)
1 small onion, minced
1/2 teaspoon salt
Salt and pepper to season
Green food coloring (optional)

Method:
· Soften the cream cheese with a spoon or with an electric mixer.
· Drain the grated cucumber in a strainer. Add the onion, cucumber, and salt to the cream cheese.
· (Optional) One drop at a time, add green food coloring until Benedictine is a pale mint green.
· Season with salt and pepper.
· Serve as a sandwich on white or whole wheat bread with lettuce.

Note: You may want to peel the cucumbers, especially if they have been waxed.

Annie used to make this often for my mother and me. It was our favorite, as a sandwich spread for lunch or on crackers for a snack.

Benedictine is a traditional Louisville dish, first popularized as a spread for the "tea sandwiches" served at ladies' luncheons. Green food coloring is often added to make the spread a pale mint green, but those of us who are benedictine purists wouldn't dare.

CHEESE COINS

YIELD: 4 DOZEN
375° OVEN

Yeah, I'm tryin' to keep on. Jus' keep a-trustin' in God and don't look back.

Ingredients:
1 **cup unsalted butter, softened**
1 **pound (4 cups) cheddar cheese, grated**
2 **cups puffed rice cereal**
2 **cups all-purpose flour**
1 **teaspoon salt**
1/8 **teaspoon cayenne pepper**

Method:
• With an electric mixer or by hand, mix the butter and cheese together.
• Sift the flour, salt, and cayenne pepper together. Add to the butter and cheese, mixing until a soft dough is formed.
• Add the puffed rice by hand or with a spoon, mixing well.
• Form 1-inch balls and flatten to make coins. Place on lightly greased baking sheets 1 inch apart.
• Bake in a 375° oven for 15 minutes, or until coins start to turn golden brown.

Grandmother kept a tin of these on hand at all times. This is the recipe she passed on to Annie.

Chicken Salad

Yield: 6 servings

Ingredients:
1 **quart cooked chicken meat (4-pound chicken, or 6 chicken breasts)**
4 **celery stalks, chopped small**
1 **cup mayonnaise**
1 **tablespoon lemon juice**
2 **teaspoons salt**
1/2 **teaspoon pepper**

Method:
· Chop the cooked chicken meat into medium-sized chunks.
· Combine the chicken with the celery in a medium-sized bowl.
· Mix the mayonnaise, lemon juice, salt, and pepper together. Add to the chicken and celery mixture. Stir until well combined.
· Season with salt and pepper.

COLE SLAW

YIELD: 6-8 SERVINGS

Ingredients:
1 **medium-size cabbage**
1 **cup mayonnaise**
2 **tablespoons white or cider vinegar**
1 **tablespoon sugar**
1 **teaspoon salt**
1/2 **teaspoon pepper**

Method:
- Wash and core the cabbage and cut it into quarters. Slice thinly from top to bottom.
- In a small bowl, combine the mayonnaise, vinegar, sugar, salt, and pepper.
- In a large bowl, toss the cabbage with the dressing.
- Season with salt and pepper.

Cooled Carrots

"I used to make cooled carrots two gallons at a time and take 'em to church. Them folks loved it, jus' ate it all up."

Yield: 8 servings

Ingredients:
5 **large carrots**
1 **medium onion**
1 **green pepper**
1 **can (10 3/4 ounces) tomato soup**
1/2 **cup salad oil**
1 **cup sugar**
3/4 **cup white or cider vinegar**
1 **teaspoon dry mustard**
1 **teaspoon salt**
1 **teaspoon pepper**

Method:
- Peel and slice the carrots into 1-inch rounds. Boil or steam until tender (about 20 minutes). Drain and cool.
- Peel the onion and cut in half, then slice into thin half circles.
- Cut the green pepper in half lengthwise and remove the seeds and white membrane. Slice each half horizontally to make thin half circles.
- Combine the soup, oil, sugar, vinegar, and spices, mixing well.
- In a mixing or serving bowl, combine the carrots, onion, and green pepper. Add the soup mixture and stir well.
- Refrigerate overnight or longer.
- Stir again before serving at room temperature.

POTATO SALAD

YIELD: 8 SERVINGS

*If you got a problem,
all you got to do is give
it to God. Let go of it
and put it at His feet.
He'll handle it in
His way, in His time.
He'll work it out.*

Ingredients:
6 **medium potatoes**
5 **celery stalks, chopped small**
1 **green pepper, chopped small** (optional)
1 1/2 **cups mayonnaise**
1 **tablespoon lemon juice**
2 **teaspoons salt**
1/2 **teaspoon pepper**
1/2 **teaspoon dry mustard**

Method:
· Boil the potatoes, whole and unpeeled, in a large pot
  of water until tender, about 30 minutes. Drain and
  cool until you are able to handle them.
· Peel and chop into 1/2-inch cubes.
· Combine the potatoes, celery, and green pepper
  (if using) in a large bowl.
· Mix the mayonnaise, lemon juice, salt, pepper, and
  dry mustard together in small bowl.
· Pour over the potatoes and combine well.

BREAD-AND-BUTTER PICKLES

YIELD: 2 QUARTS

Ingredients:
2 quarts pickling cucumbers, sliced in 1/4-inch rounds
6 small onions, halved and sliced
1/4 cup salt
water and ice
2 cups white or cider vinegar
2 cups sugar
3/4 teaspoon tumeric
1/2 teaspoon ground cloves
1/2 teaspoon celery seeds
1 teaspoon mustard seeds

Method:
• Soak the cucumbers and onions in enough salted ice water to cover for 3-4 hours.
• In a large non reactive pot, bring the vinegar, sugar, and spices to a boil.
• Drain the cucumbers and onions before adding to the pot. Simmer covered until the cucumbers are tender.
• When cool, place in glass jars and refrigerate.

CHOW CHOW

YIELD: 2 QUARTS

Ingredients:
4 **medium onions, chopped small**
1 **cabbage, shredded**
5 **green tomatoes, chopped medium**
4 **hot peppers, seeded, chopped small**
2 **red bell peppers, seeded, chopped small**
3 **cups white or cider vinegar**
2 **cups sugar**
1 **tablespoon salt**

Method:
• Place the onion and the cabbage in a large pot.
  Add 1 cup of water and cook covered for about
  10-15 minutes until they start to become tender.
• Add all the other ingredients and stir well. Cook
  about 1 1/2 hours.
• Season to taste.
• When cool, place in glass jars and refrigerate.

Fruit Punch

Yield: 1 1/2 gallons

Ingredients:
2 **cans (32 ounce) tropical punch**
1 **can (12 ounce) frozen lemonade concentrate**
2 **quarts water**
2 **cans (16 ounce) fruit salad**
1 **bottle (1 liter) lemon lime soda at
room temperature**

Method:
- In a large container, combine the tropical punch, lemonade concentrate, water, and fruit salad. Stir well.
- Freeze in a container (or containers) that will fit into the punch bowl you will use to serve the punch.
- Take the punch out of the freezer 30 minutes before serving.
- Unmold block(s) of frozen punch into punch bowl and pour the lemon lime soda over it.

SPICE TEA

YIELD: 1 GALLON

Sometimes if you hold your peace, you do better. 'Causin' if you argue back, that's the way folks get to fightin'. They jus' argue back and argue back at one 'nother. And one of 'em end up losin'. So I done learn't how to keep my mouth shut.

Ingredients:
4 large (family size) black tea bags
2 teaspoons allspice
2 teaspoons cloves
2 teaspoons cinnamon
3 quarts boiling water
1 cup sugar
6-ounce can frozen orange juice concentrate
1 cup lemon juice
1/2 liter ginger ale

Method:
· Place the allspice, cloves, and cinnamon with the tea bags in a large container and pour boiling water over them.
· Let it steep for 3-5 minutes. Strain and set aside to cool.
· When the tea has cooled, add the orange and lemon juices and ginger ale.
· Serve chilled over ice.

Dinner

DINNER

MEATS

Barbecue Pork

Barbecue Ribs

Chicken and Dumplin's

Chicken Pot Pie

Fried Chicken and Gravy

Chili

Fried Catfish

Meat Loaf

Oxtails

Stuffed Green Peppers

Turkey and Gravy

Turkey Hash

SAUCES

Barbecue Sauce

Tomato Sauce

My grandmother had the preacher over to the house once't a month on a Sunday, and she'd have all these other folks over ever' time he come. The grown folks got to eat first and then the children ate last. I stood there durin' the whole meal, fannin' the flies with a peach branch.

When them grown folks got through eatin', there weren't no chicken or nothin' left. They sat there and ate up all the food, everthin' on the table. So one day I 'member I slipped in there early and got me a chicken breast and went up under the house and ate it. I got caught and got the worst whuppin'. But I didn't care—I was full of chicken.

BARBECUE PORK

YIELD: 6-8 SERVINGS
350° OVEN

*Just keep on livin'.
You live and learn,
then forget it all when
you die.*

Ingredients:
3 **pounds boneless pork shoulder**
1 **cup plus** 2 **cups barbecue sauce** (see recipe page 99)

Method:
• In a roasting pan covered with foil, bake the pork shoulder in a 350° oven until it reaches an internal temperature of 140° and is tender. Take out of the oven and cut into 2-inch squares.
• Pour 1 cup of the barbecue sauce over the pork and put it back in the oven to cook for 30 minutes, stirring occasionally.
• Remove the pork from the oven and, using two forks, shred the squares into strands.
• Add the remaining 2 cups of barbecue sauce and mix well.
• Season with salt and pepper.
• Reheat, if necessary, and serve on buns.

BARBECUE RIBS

YIELD: 6 SERVINGS
350° OVEN

Ingredients:
6 pounds baby back ribs
Salt and pepper
4 cups barbecue sauce (see recipe page 99)

Method:
· Rinse the ribs and season with salt and pepper.
· In a roasting pan covered with foil, bake the ribs in a 350° oven until the meat is tender, about 45 minutes.
· Baste the ribs really well with the barbecue sauce. Put them back in the oven for 30 minutes, turning and basting every 10 minutes to make sure they are evenly coated.
· Heat any remaining barbecue sauce and serve with the ribs.

Chicken and Dumplin's

"Miz Rankin used to ast me to make this ever' week. Chicken 'n' dumplin's, greens, and hot water cornbread—just like we had for dinner in the country. She loved 'em."

Yield: 6 servings

I been at this cookin' since I was a chile, and I'm eighty years old.

Ingredients:
1 **chicken (3-4 pounds), whole or pieces**
Salt and pepper
3 **cups all-purpose flour**
1/2 **cup solid vegetable shortening**
3/4 **cup water**
Additional flour for rolling

Method:
• Rinse the chicken under cold water. Put in large pot and fill with enough water to cover. Bring to a boil and skim the foam off the top. Simmer, adding water if necessary, for about 1-1 1/2 hours until chicken is tender and falling off the bone.
• Turn off the heat and remove the chicken from the pot. Strain and season the stock.
• When the chicken is cool enough to handle, debone and tear the meat into bite-sized pieces. Put this aside.
• Sift the flour into a medium-sized bowl. Make a well in the flour and put the solid vegetable shortening in the well. Slowly work the shortening into the flour with your fingers. Gradually add the water while working shortening and flour together until dough is stiff enough to roll out.

- Flour a rolling surface and, working with manageable amounts, roll the dough out to a thickness of 1/16 inch. Cut the dough into long strips 1 1/2 inches wide.
- Bring 2 quarts of the chicken stock to a boil and, working with one strip at a time, pinch off 2-inch lengths of dough and drop these into the boiling stock.
- Pause occasionally to stir the dumplin's.
- Keep rolling, cutting, and pinching until the stock is full of dumplin's. Cook for 20 minutes
- Add the chicken to the stock. Stir and season with salt and pepper.

Chicken Pot Pie

"This here recipe takes some time to make, but it's worth every minute of it. Most people never had homemade chicken pot pie. It's the best."

Yield: 8 servings
350° oven

It's 'cordin' to the way you feel. 'Nother person don't know how you feel. So you got to tell 'em. Do your part and let them worry about the rest.

Ingredients:
1 **chicken** (3-4 **pounds**)**, whole or pieces**
3 **carrots, peeled and cubed**
2 **tablespoons plus 4 tablespoons solid vegetable shortening**
1 **medium onion, chopped small**
3 **celery stalks, chopped small**
1 **cup peas, frozen, fresh or 8 1/2 ounce can drained**
1/2 **cup all-purpose flour**
1 **recipe of pie crust, in dough form** (see recipe page 132)

Method:
· Rinse the chicken under cold water. Put in large pot and fill with enough water to cover. Bring to a boil and skim the foam off the top. Simmer, adding water if necessary, for about 1-1 1/2 hours until chicken is very tender and falling off the bone.
· Turn off the heat and remove the chicken from the pot. Strain and season the stock with salt and pepper.
· When the chicken is cool enough to handle, debone and tear the meat into bite-sized pieces. Put this aside.
· Bring the stock to a boil and cook the carrots in the stock until tender. Remove the carrots with a slotted spoon and add to the reserved chicken. Set both aside.

- Heat 2 tablespoons of the shortening in a skillet over medium heat. Cook the onion and the celery until tender and add to the reserved chicken.
- Heat the remaining 4 tablespoons of shortening in the skillet. Stir the flour into the oil and cook on low heat, slowly adding 4 cups of the stock, one cup at a time. Stir constantly. Bring to a boil and simmer for 10 minutes.
- Pour the thickened stock over the chicken. Add the peas and mix all the ingredients together well.
- Spoon into a shallow, rectangular 2-quart baking dish.
- Roll out pie dough in a shape larger than the baking dish. Lay the dough over the top and trim to the edge of the pan. Flute or press with the tines of a fork to make a decorative edge.
- Cut vents in the crust to allow steam to escape and place pie on a baking sheet.
- Bake on the bottom rack of a 350° oven for 30 minutes, or until the chicken mixture starts to bubble. Move the pie to the top rack for 8-10 minutes until the crust browns.

Fried Chicken and Gravy

"See, you put your flour in the bag. Shake some paprika down in there. Then you need some black pepper and salt. Now…need to put the larger pieces in first. Put that breast and the thick part of the leg in first. Start fryin' it skin side up—so it don't stick. You check it by liftin' up the piece and lookin' under. This all takes longer than you think. You can't rush them big pieces. See, you can't turn it up too high, so you got to stay with it and watch so it don't burn."

Yield: 8 servings

I try to treat people the way I wants to be treated. That's why the Lord bless me so.

Ingredients:
2 **chickens** (6-8 **pounds**), **cut into pieces**
Salt and pepper
2 **cups all-purpose flour**
1 **teaspoon black pepper**
1 **teaspoon paprika**
2 **teaspoons salt**
Solid vegetable shortening or oil
3 **tablespoons all-purpose flour** (or use leftover seasoned flour)
2 **cups chicken stock**

Method:
• Wash and season the chicken pieces with salt and pepper.
• Combine the flour, black pepper, paprika, and 2 teaspoons of salt in a flat bottom dish or plastic bag.
• Heat 1/2 inch of oil in a skillet until hot.

- Coat both sides of each chicken piece with the flour mixture and fry, "skin side up" first and then turn over, until the chicken is tender and golden brown on both sides. This will take about 20 minutes per piece.
- Lay the fried chicken on paper towels to drain off the excess oil.
- Pour off the fat from the pan, leaving only a little fat (about 3 tablespoons) and the browned flour from the chicken.
- Over medium heat, add the remaining 3 tablespoons of flour (or the same amount of seasoned flour) to the pan and stir well.
- Add the chicken stock, stirring continuously, and cook for at least 10 minutes to cook out the taste of the flour.
- If the gravy gets too thick, add a little water. If it is too thin, let it simmer so that some of the water evaporates.
- Season the gravy with salt and pepper and strain if desired.

CHILI

YIELD: 6 SERVINGS

You got to be friendly to make friends. Some people don't know how to make friends. You got to help 'em learn how, by bein' friendly to them. That helps 'em learn.

Ingredients:
2 **tablespoons solid vegetable shortening or oil**
1 **medium onion, chopped small**
1 **green pepper, chopped small** (optional)
2 **pounds ground beef**
3 **cups** (28-ounce can) **tomato puree or crushed tomatoes**
1 **can** (6-ounce can) **tomato paste**
4 **cups** (two 19-ounce cans) **kidney beans, including liquid**
1 **tablespoon chili powder**
1 **teaspoon ground cumin**
1 **teaspoon salt**
1 **teaspoon pepper**

Method:
- Heat the shortening or oil in the bottom of a large soup pot. Cook the onion and green pepper over low heat until tender.
- Turn the heat up to medium and add the ground beef. Stir and cook until well done. Drain off any excess fat.
- Add the tomato puree, tomato paste, kidney beans, chili powder, cumin, salt, and pepper. Stir to combine.
- If necessary, add water so that all the ingredients are covered. Simmer for 40 minutes.
- Adjust seasoning.

Note: This recipe calls for less salt to balance the salt in the kidney beans.

Fried Catfish

Yield: 6 servings

God is good. The Lord, He lookin' out all around me.

Ingredients:
2 pounds catfish filets (6 large or 12 small)
2 eggs
1/4 cup milk
1 1/2 cups white cornmeal
1/2 cup all-purpose flour
2 teaspoons salt
1 teaspoon black pepper
1/2 teaspoon cayenne pepper
Solid vegetable shortening or oil

Method:
- Rinse the catfish and dry with paper towels.
- Beat the eggs and the milk together in a large flat dish.
- In a second flat dish, combine the cornmeal, flour, and spices.
- In a skillet, heat 1/4 inch of oil or shortening.
- Dip the catfish into the egg mixture and then into the cornmeal, coating well on both sides.
- Fry for about 2 minutes on each side.
- Serve with tartar sauce.

Meat Loaf

Yield: 8 servings
350° oven

Ingredients:
2 pounds ground beef
4 eggs
1 cup oatmeal or bread crumbs
1 onion, chopped small
1 green pepper, chopped small
2 cups plus 1 cup tomato sauce (see recipe page 100)
1 tablespoon salt
1 teaspoon black pepper

Method:
- Combine all the ingredients (reserving 1 cup of the tomato sauce) and mix well.
- Shape into a 13x6-inch loaf and place in a 13-inch long glass baking pan.
- Brush with tomato sauce and add 1/2 inch water on either side of the loaf.
- Bake in a 350° oven for 1 hour, or until the meat loaf reaches an internal temperature of 150°, basting (with the juices) during cooking.
- Take the meat loaf out of the oven and cover with the remaining cup of tomato sauce. Cool for 20 minutes, slice and serve.

Variation:
Meat loaf can also be baked in a 9x4-inch loaf pan. Omit the added water and basting. The cooking time may be a little longer.

OXTAILS

"I don't know why they call it oxtails, 'causin' it's really the tail of the cow."

YIELD: 6 SERVINGS

Ingredients:
1 **small onion, sliced**
6 **pounds oxtails**
1 **tablespoon salt**
Salt and pepper

Method:
· Rinse the oxtails in cold water.
· Place the onion with the oxtails in a medium-sized pot and cover with water. Add the salt and bring to a boil.
· Reduce the heat and simmer for 3 1/2-4 hours. The oxtails are done when the meat is tender and starts to fall off the bone.
· Season with salt and pepper.

Note: Serve with hot water cornbread and greens.

STUFFED GREEN PEPPERS

"This is Mr. Rankin's favorite. I make up a whole lot at a time and put 'em in the freezer so he can have one whenever he wants."

YIELD: 6 SERVINGS
        350° OVEN

Ingredients:
6 **green peppers**
2 **tablespoons oil**
1 **medium onion, chopped**
2 **pounds ground beef**
2 **cups plus** 1 **cup tomato sauce** (see recipe page 100)
1 **teaspoon salt**
1/4 **teaspoon pepper**

Method:
- Slice the tops off the green peppers 1/2 inch below the top ridge. Chop the tops of the peppers into small cubes, discarding the stems, and reserve.
- Remove the seeds and the white membrane from the inside of the peppers, being careful not to harm the sides.
- Cover the peppers with water in a pan and bring to a boil. Reduce the heat and simmer until tender. (You may need to weight the peppers with a smaller lid to keep them submerged while cooking.) When the peppers are tender, take them out of the water and set aside to cool.
- Heat the oil in a skillet and cook the reserved green pepper and the onion until tender. Add the ground beef and cook until well done. Drain off any excess fat.

- Add 2 cups of the tomato sauce to the beef. Combine well, and season with salt and pepper.
- Fill the green peppers with the meat and tomato mixture and place them in a baking pan, touching so that they hold each other upright.
- Spoon the remaining cup of tomato sauce over the peppers.
- Bake in a 350° oven for 20-30 minutes.

Variation:

Add 2 cups of cooked rice or pasta (1 cup uncooked) to the meat mixture before stuffing the peppers. This allows you to cut back on the amount of beef by 1/4 pound, or make enough filling for 1-2 additional pepper(s).

Turkey and Gravy

Yield: 14–18 servings
450° oven

When you help others,
God just opens up and
takes care of you.

Ingredients:
1 (14–18 pound) turkey
Salt and pepper
Paprika
1 green pepper, cut in half with the seeds and
  membrane removed
1 whole onion, peeled and cut in half
3 stalks celery, washed and cut in thirds
1 cup unsalted butter, melted
1/2 cup all-purpose flour, sifted

Method:
- Remove the neck and the giblets from inside the bird.
- Simmer in 1 quart of water until about 3/4 of a quart of the liquid remains. Strain and reserve the stock.
- Rinse the turkey inside and out and stand it on end to drain for a few minutes.
- Place the turkey in the roaster pan and season the inside with salt, pepper, and paprika. Season the turkey outside, starting with the breast, then the sides, and, finally, the top.
- Place the cut green pepper, onion, and celery inside the turkey.
- Fold wings back and under the turkey. With a tooth pick fasten the skin together at breast opening. Tie the drum sticks together with string.
- Pour the melted butter over the turkey, rubbing it, with the seasoning, into the skin on the top and sides.
- Make a foil "hood" that is large enough to cover the turkey without touching it.

- Bake in a 450° oven for 30 minutes. Turn oven down to 350° for the remaining cooking time.*Halfway through the cooking time, remove the foil and baste the turkey with the pan drippings. Return to the oven uncovered.
- Move the turkey to a carving board to rest for 20 minutes before cutting.
- Scrape the bottom of the roasting pan to loosen any particles. Unless you have a flat-bottom roasting pan, pour the roasting liquid into a skillet.
- Over medium heat, stir 1/2 cup flour into the turkey juices, stirring well to get any lumps out. Cook for a few minutes while stirring.
- Add the stock gradually, stirring. Cook until thickened.
- Season with salt and pepper. Straining is optional.

Figure 1 pound of turkey per person.

*Cooking Times
  Under 16 pounds—15 minutes per pound
  Over 16 pounds—12 minutes per pound

  Breast meat—170°
  Thigh meat—185°

Turkey Hash

"I used to make this up the day after Thanksgiving. Had it for dinner with corncakes and biscuits."

Yield: 6 servings

Ingredients:
2 tablespoons vegetable oil
1 small onion
2 medium potatoes, peeled and cut into small cubes
2-4 cups cooked turkey, shredded
2 teaspoons salt
1/2 teaspoon pepper

Method:
• In a medium-sized pot, heat the oil and cook the onion until tender.
• Add the potatoes with just enough water to cover. Simmer until the potatoes are tender, about 20 minutes.
• Add the turkey, salt, and pepper and simmer for another 30 minutes.

BARBECUE SAUCE

YIELD: 1 QUART

Ingredients:
3 cups (28-ounce can) tomato puree
1 cup water
1 small onion, chopped small
1/2 cup brown sugar, firmly packed
1/2 cup unsalted butter
1/4 cup Worcestershire sauce
1/2 cup cider vinegar
1/2 teaspoon hot sauce
1/2 teaspoon salt

Method:
· Combine all the ingredients in a saucepan. Bring to a
  boil, stirring occasionally.
· Reduce heat and simmer for 20 minutes.
· Season with salt and pepper.

TOMATO SAUCE

YIELD: 3 CUPS

You got to believe in somethin' for it to help you.

Ingredients:
1/4 **cup solid vegetable shortening or oil**
1 **medium onion, chopped small**
3 **cups (28-ounce can) tomato puree**
1 **cup water**
1/4 **cup brown sugar**
2 **tablespoons white or cider vinegar**
2 **teaspoons salt**

Method:
• Heat the oil in large skillet and cook the onion
  until soft.
• Add the tomato puree, water, brown sugar, vinegar,
  and salt.
• Simmer for 40 minutes stirring occasionally.
• Taste and adjust the seasoning

Cakes and Icings

Cakes and Icings

Cakes
Apple Cake
Buttermilk Pound Cake
Blackberry Jam Cake
Chocolate Cake
Chocolate Pound Cake
Hummingbird Cake
German Cake
Gingerbread
Pineapple Upside Down Cake
Plum Spice Cake
Sour Cream Pound Cake
Yellow Cake

Icing
Caramel Icing
Chocolate Icing
Coconut Icing
Coconut Pecan Icing
Cream Cheese Icing

I got a list of names of sick people I call 'bout twice't a week, jus' different ones from my church. I do the best I can with it. There's an ol' lady I been callin'. She's ninety somethin' years old. Her grandson's with her. He's takin' care of her. He said he couldn't understand why he retired, but the Lord showed him he had to take care his grandmother.

It's so sweet. I am so glad I take up time with that lady. It jus' make me feel good, bless her heart. She don't know me, but I know her. I used to see her at church, when her husband was livin'.

When me and Jack was able, we went to see about people. You know, that is why the Lord's blessin' me so. Do unto others as you'd have them to do unto you. Treat people like you want to be treated.

CAKES

It was a special treat when Annie made a cake—any cake. They were always from scratch, always three layers, and always delicious. On the subject of cake mix she says, *"Ain't nothin' but some ol' box cake. Who'd a want that?"* Try one of these recipes and you will agree!

Cake baking is both a magical art and an exact science. It is important to measure the ingredients carefully and not take any shortcuts.

PAN PREPARATION

We recommend preparing the pans by first coating them with a thin layer of shortening or butter and sprinkling with flour.

CREAMING BUTTER AND SUGAR

The butter needs to be at room temperature. A mixer works best to cream the butter and sugar together. Annie always beats the two together until they become paler in color and light and airy. This process takes about two to three minutes.

ADDITION OF WET AND DRY INGREDIENTS

According to Annie, it is important to mix all the ingredients together in a way that produces the smoothest batter. In order to keep the flour from forming lumps when mixed with the liquid, she adds the flour and the liquid alternately, starting and ending with flour. Start by adding half of the flour to the creamed butter mixture and mix until well combined. Then add all the liquid and mix until well combined. Lastly, add the remaining flour and again mix until well combined.

CHECKING FOR DONENESS

Always start checking the cake for doneness 5-10 minutes before the time on the recipe. Insert a toothpick in the center of the cake. The cake is ready when the toothpick comes out without any batter clinging to it.

COOLING

Cool the cake in the pan and on a rack for 10 minutes. After running a knife around the edge, you can turn it out onto the rack to finish cooling. Put an upside down rack over the top of the cake pan. While holding the two together, flip the cake pan and rack. Allow the cake layer to cool completely.

ICING

Annie starts with the first layer turned upside down on the serving plate and then ices its top. The second layer is put on next, right-side up and it's top is iced. The third layer goes on last, right-side up. Then the cake sides are iced, making sure to leave plenty of icing for the top. Annie ices the top last, covering it with decorative peaks.

STORING

Cakes keep well stored in an airtight container at room temperature. If the icing has been cooked it is recommended that you store the cake in the refrigerator. The pound cakes, well wrapped, are the most suitable for freezing.

APPLE CAKE

YIELD: 1 BUNDT OR TUBE CAKE
350° OVEN

You and me would make

us a good cafeteria.

Ingredients:
3 **cups all-purpose flour**
2 **teaspoons baking soda**
1/2 **teaspoon salt**
1/2 **teaspoon cinnamon**
1/2 **teaspoon allspice**
1/2 **teaspoon nutmeg**
1/2 **teaspoon cloves**
2 **cups sugar**
1 **cup unsalted butter, melted**
2 **eggs, lightly beaten**
4 **apples, chopped into small cubes**
1 **cup chopped pecans**
powdered sugar

Method:
- Grease a bundt or tube pan.
- Sift the flour, baking soda, salt, spices, and sugar into the bowl of an electric mixer. Combine well.
- On low setting, stir in the melted butter and beaten eggs. Mix until well combined.
- Fold in the chopped apples and pecans by hand.
- Pour into a greased bundt or tube pan.
- Bake in 350° oven for 1 hour or until a toothpick comes out clean.
- Allow to cool for 10 minutes, run a knife around the edge, and turn out onto a rack to continue cooling.
- Sprinkle with powdered sugar before serving.

Buttermilk Pound Cake

Yield: 1 bundt, tube, or loaf cake
350° oven

Ingredients:

1 **cup unsalted butter, softened**

2 **cups sugar**

4 **eggs**

1 **teaspoon vanilla extract**

1/2 **teaspoon lemon extract**

3 **cups all-purpose flour**

1/2 **teaspoon baking soda**

1/2 **teaspoon baking powder**

1/2 **teaspoon salt**

1 **cup buttermilk**

Powdered sugar

Method:

· Grease and flour the cake pan.

· Cream the butter and sugar together until light and fluffy.

· Add the eggs one at a time, beating well after each.

· Sift the flour, baking soda, baking powder, and salt
  together. With the mixer on low, add the flour in thirds to
  the mixture, alternating with half the buttermilk after each
  addition of flour. Mix just until blended.

· Add the lemon and vanilla extracts.

· Pour the batter into the pan.

· Bake in a 350° oven for 1 hour and 10 minutes or until a
  toothpick comes out clean.

· Allow to cool for 10 minutes, then run a knife around
  the edge and turn out onto a rack to cool completely.

· Sprinkle with powdered sugar before serving.

*Note: This recipe almost didn't make it in the book. It was written on a piece of
paper and tucked away in a drawer, and Annie couldn't find it. She kept telling me
how good it was and how she used to make it all the time. As we were in the editing
phase of the book, she found it and called me with it.*

BLACKBERRY JAM CAKE

"I make this at Christmas for my family. You can leave the raisins and nuts out, 'causin' some folks don't like 'em. The blackberry jam can be with or without seeds—don't make no difference, lessen you mind seeds in your cake."

YIELD: 1 THREE-LAYER OR TUBE CAKE
325° OVEN

You can use margarine, but it's better to use butter. Butter gives it some different flavor.

Ingredients:
1 **cup butter, softened**
1 **cup brown sugar**
5 **eggs, separated**
3 **cups all-purpose flour**
1 **teaspoon baking soda**
1 **teaspoon cinnamon**
1 **teaspoon nutmeg**
1 **teaspoon cloves**
1 **teaspoon allspice**
1 **cup buttermilk**
1 1/2 **cups blackberry jam**
1 **cup chopped pecans**
1 **cup raisins** (optional)
1/2 **cup bourbon** (optional)
Wax paper for lining pan(s)

Method:
• Grease three 8- or 9-inch cake pans or 1 tube pan.
  Line the bottom(s) with wax (or parchment) paper.
  Flour the sides.
• Cream the butter and sugar together until light
  and fluffy.

- Add the eggs, beating well after each.
- Sift the flour, baking soda, and spices together.
- Add the flour and the buttermilk to the mixture alternately, starting and ending with flour. Mix well after each addition.
- Add the blackberry jam and mix well.
- Fold in the pecans and raisins. (optional)
- Pour into lined baking pans.
- Bake in a 325° oven for 25 minutes or until a toothpick comes out clean.
- Allow to cool for 10 minutes, then run a knife around the edge of the pans, and turn the cakes out onto racks.
- If you are using bourbon, dribble bourbon over the cakes at this time.
- When cool, frost with caramel icing (see recipe page 123).

CHOCOLATE CAKE

It don't matter how you decorate it, you gonna cut and eat it anyway.

Ingredients:
1 **cup unsweetened cocoa, sifted**
2 **cups boiling water**
1 **cup unsalted butter, softened**
2 1/2 **cups sugar**
4 **eggs**
1 1/2 **teaspoons vanilla extract**
2 3/4 **cups all-purpose flour**
2 **teaspoons baking soda**
1/2 **teaspoon baking powder**
1/2 **teaspoon salt**

Method:
· Grease and flour 3 round 8- or 9-inch cake pans.
· Combine the sifted cocoa and boiling water, stirring until smooth, and set aside to cool.
· Cream the butter and sugar together with an electric mixer until light and fluffy.
· Add the eggs one at a time, mixing well after each.
· Add the vanilla extract and mix well.
· Sift the flour, baking soda, and baking powder together.
· On a low setting, add the flour and the cocoa mixture alternately, starting and ending with flour. Mix until well combined, being careful not to overmix.
· Pour the batter into the cake pans.
· Bake in a 350° oven for 25-30 minutes or until a toothpick comes out clean.
· Allow to cool for 10 minutes, then run a knife around the edge of the pans and turn out onto racks.
· Frost when completely cool.

CHOCOLATE POUND CAKE

YIELD: 1 BUNDT CAKE
325° OVEN

Ingredients:
1 1/2 **cups unsalted butter, softened**
3 **cups sugar**
5 **eggs**
3 **cups all-purpose flour**
1/2 **cup unsweetened cocoa**
1/4 **teaspoon baking powder**
1/2 **teaspoon salt**
1 **cup milk**
1 **teaspoon vanilla extract**
powdered sugar

Method:
· Grease and flour a 9-inch bundt or tube pan.
· Cream the butter and sugar together until light and fluffy.
· Add the eggs one at a time, beating after each one.
· Sift together the flour, cocoa, baking powder, and salt.
· Add the flour and the milk to the butter mixture
  alternately, starting and ending with flour.
· Pour into the pan.
· Bake in a 325° oven for 1 1/2 hours or until a
  toothpick comes out clean.
· Allow to cool for 10 minutes, then run a knife around
  the edge of the pan and turn out onto a rack to
  cool completely.
· Sprinkle with powdered sugar before serving.

HUMMINGBIRD CAKE

YIELD: 1 THREE-LAYER CAKE
350° OVEN

I leave the butter out at night if I'm gonna bake a cake the next day. I leave it out so it be soft. See, 'causin' you not supposed to melt butter to make a cake. It makes it tough.

Cake Ingredients:
3 **cups all-purpose flour**
2 **cups sugar**
1 **teaspoon baking soda**
1 **teaspoon salt**
1 **teaspoon cinnamon**
3 **eggs, beaten**
1 **cup vegetable oil**
1 1/2 **teaspoons vanilla extract**
8 **ounce can of crushed pineapple, with juice**
1 **cup pecans chopped**
2 **bananas, chopped**

Icing:
Cream cheese icing (see recipe page 127)
1/2 **cup chopped pecans**

Method:
· Grease and flour 3 round 8- or 9-inch cake pans.
· Sift the flour, sugar, soda, salt, and cinnamon into a
  medium-sized bowl.
· Add the eggs and oil, stirring with a spoon by hand,
  until the ingredients are well combined. Do not beat.
· Stir in the vanilla extract, pineapple (and its juice),
  pecans, and bananas.
· Spoon into the pans.
· Bake in a 350° oven for 25-30 minutes, or until a
  toothpick comes out clean.

- Allow to cool for 10 minutes, then run a knife around the edge of the pans, and turn out onto racks.
- When completely cool, frost the cake with cream cheese icing (see recipe page 127) and sprinkle the top with pecans.

This is a very traditional southern cake. Annie learned this recipe at my mother's request.

GERMAN CAKE

"Miz. Rankin loved that German cake, told me it was her daddy's favorite."

YIELD: 1 THREE-LAYER CAKE
350° OVEN

Ingredients:
4 ounces semisweet chocolate, chopped
1/2 cup boiling water
2 cups sugar
1 cup unsalted butter, softened
2 teaspoons vanilla extract
4 eggs, separated
2 1/2 cups all-purpose flour
1 teaspoon baking soda
1/2 teaspoon salt
1 cup buttermilk

Method:
· Grease and flour 3 round 8- or 9-inch cake pans
· Chop the chocolate into small pieces. Place in a sauce pan and pour 1/2 cup boiling water over the chocolate. Let it sit, then stir and heat on low if needed to melt. Set aside to cool.
· Cream the butter and sugar together until light and fluffy.
· Add the egg yolks one at a time, beating well after each one.
· Add the vanilla and melted chocolate.
· Sift the flour, baking soda, and salt together. Add the flour and the buttermilk to the chocolate mixture alternately, starting and ending with flour.

- Pour into the cake pans.
- Bake in a 350° oven for 25-30 minutes, or until a toothpick comes out clean.
- Allow to cool for 10 minutes, then run a knife around the edge of the pans and turn out onto racks.
- Frost when completely cool with Coconut Pecan Icing (see recipe page 126).

GINGERBREAD

YIELD: ONE 9x12-INCH GINGERBREAD
350° OVEN

Ingredients for Gingerbread:
1 **cup unsalted butter, melted**
2 **cups sugar**
1/4 **cup molasses**
2 **teaspoons ground ginger**
2 **teaspoons cinnamon**
1 **teaspoon cloves**
1 **teaspoon nutmeg**
2 **cups buttermilk**
2 **eggs, beaten**
3 **cups all-purpose flour**
2 **teaspoons baking soda**
1/2 **teaspoon salt**

Ingredients for Lemon Sauce:
1 **cup sugar**
2 **tablespoons flour**
2 **tablespoons lemon juice**
1/2 **cup hot water**
1/2 **cup unsalted butter**

Method for Gingerbread:
· Grease and flour a 9x12x2-inch pan.
· Combine the butter, sugar, molasses, and spices, mixing well.
· Add the buttermilk and the eggs and mix well.
· Sift the flour, baking soda, and salt together.
· Add flour and mix until well blended.

- Pour the cake batter into the prepared pan.
- Bake in a 350° oven for 45 minutes, or until a toothpick comes out clean.
- Allow to cool for 10 minutes, then run a knife around the edge of the pan. Turn out onto a rack or place pan on a rack to cool completely.

Method for Lemon Sauce:
- In a small saucepan combine the flour, sugar, and salt.
- While stirring continuously over medium heat, add the lemon juice and water.
- Add the butter and stir until it is melted and the sauce begins to thicken. It is ready when it reaches the consistency of syrup.
- Pour the warm lemon sauce over the gingerbread just before serving.

PINEAPPLE UPSIDE DOWN CAKE

YIELD: ONE 10-INCH ROUND SKILLET CAKE
350° OVEN

When you checkin' the cake, don't mash it with your finger. It makes the cake go down hard. Use a toothpick.

Topping Ingredients (make first):
1/2 **cup unsalted butter**
1/2 **cup brown sugar**
20-ounce can sliced pineapple (7-8 slices)

Cake Ingredients:
1/2 **cup butter, softened**
1 **cup sugar**
2 **eggs**
2 **cups all-purpose flour**
1 **teaspoon baking powder**
1 **teaspoon vanilla extract**
2/3 **cup milk**

Method for topping:
· In a 10-inch cast iron skillet, melt the butter. Add the brown sugar and cook on low heat, stirring constantly until the sugar dissolves. (The grainy texture leaves and the melted butter combines with the sugar.) This will take five minutes or more.
· Remove from the heat.
· Arrange pineapple slices in the sugar mixture.

Method for cake:

- With an electric mixer, cream the butter and sugar.
- Add the eggs one at a time, beating well after each.
- Sift the flour and the baking powder together.
- Add the flour and the milk to the mixture alternately, starting and ending with flour.
- Pour the mixture over the pineapple slices and sugar mixture in skillet.
- Bake in a 350° oven for 40-45 minutes, or until the cake is golden brown on top, or an inserted toothpick comes out clean.
- Run a knife around the edge of the pan. Then, holding a large serving plate upside down over the skillet, turn the skillet and plate upside down. After the cake drops out, wait for a minute to let the brown sugar sauce drip down the sides before removing the skillet.

Note: You will need a serving plate bigger than the top of the skillet. If you do not have a skillet, this cake can be made in an 8x8-inch square pan. Cook the sugar and the butter in a pan on the stove and then pour the mixture around pineapple slices that have been arranged in a greased cake pan.

PLUM SPICE CAKE

"This cake jus' come to me in my head."

YIELD: 1 BUNDT CAKE
350° OVEN

Ingredients:
2 **cups all-purpose flour**
2 1/2 **teaspoons baking powder**
1 **teaspoon cinnamon**
1 **teaspoon cloves**
1 **cup vegetable oil**
2 **cups sugar**
3 **eggs**
2 **(4-ounce) jars of pureed babyfood plums**
1 **cup chopped walnuts or pecans**
Powdered sugar

Method:
· Grease and flour a tube or bundt pan.
· Sift together the flour, baking powder, cinnamon, and cloves.
· In a large mixing bowl, combine the oil, sugar, eggs, and plums. Mix well.
· Add the flour mixture and mix together well.
· Stir in the chopped nuts.
· Pour the mixture into the pan.
· Bake in a 350° degree oven for 50-60 minutes, or until a toothpick comes out clean.
· Allow the cake to cool for 10 minutes, then run a knife around the edge of the pan and turn it out onto a rack to cool completely.
· Sprinkle with powdered sugar before serving.

SOUR CREAM POUND CAKE

"This pound cake is my favorite. I slice 'em up and put 'em in the freezer."

YIELD: 1 BUNDT CAKE
325° OVEN

Ingredients:
1 **cup unsalted butter, softened**
3 **cups sugar**
6 **eggs**
3 **cups all-purpose flour**
1/4 **teaspoon baking soda**
1/2 **teaspoon salt**
1 **cup sour cream**
1 **teaspoon vanilla extract**
1 **teaspoon lemon extract**
powdered sugar

Method:
• Grease and flour a bundt or tube pan.
• Cream the butter and sugar together until light and fluffy.
• Add the eggs one at a time, beating well after each addition.
• Sift the flour, baking soda, and salt together.
• Add the flour and the sour cream alternately to the batter, starting and ending with flour. Mix only until blended.
• Add the vanilla and lemon extracts.
• Pour the batter into the baking pan.
• Bake in a 325° oven for 1 hour and 20 minutes, or until a toothpick inserted in the center comes out clean.
• Allow the cake to cool in the pan for 10 minutes, then run a knife around the edge and turn it out onto a rack to cool completely.
• Sprinkle with powdered sugar before serving.

YELLOW CAKE

YIELD: 1 THREE-LAYER CAKE
350° OVEN

That's all I made—three layer cakes for your birthday. Every time you had a birthday. Made cakes for all four of you and sometimes for Mr. and Mrs. Rankin.

Ingredients:
1 **cup unsalted butter, softened**
2 **cups sugar**
3 **cups all-purpose flour**
2 **teaspoons baking powder**
4 **eggs, separated**
1 **cup milk**
1/2 **teaspoon lemon extract**
1 **teaspoon vanilla extract**

Method:
· Grease and flour 3 round 8-or 9-inch cake pans.
· Sift the flour and baking powder together.
· Beat the egg whites until stiff.
· Cream the butter and sugar together until light and fluffy.
· Add the egg yolks, one at a time, beating after each.
· Add the flour and the milk to the mixture alternately, starting and ending with flour.
· Add the lemon and vanilla extracts and fold in the egg whites.
· Pour into the pans.
· Bake in a 350° oven for 25-30 minutes or until a toothpick comes out clean.
· Cool the cakes in the pans for 10 minutes, then run a knife around the edge of the pans and turn out onto racks. Cool completely before icing.

Recommended icings:
Caramel (see recipe page 123), Chocolate (see recipe page 124), Coconut (see recipe page 125)

Annie calls this "One, Two, Three Cake"— one cup butter, two cups sugar, three cups flour.

CARAMEL ICING

"Used to be, you cooked sugar with butter and milk to make caramel icing. I don't do that no more. This is the easy way to make it. That powdered sugar is better than that other. It makes it easier."

YIELD: ICING FOR 1 THREE-LAYER CAKE

Ingredients:
2 1/2 cups powdered sugar
2 cups brown sugar
1/2 teaspoon salt
3/4 cup unsalted butter, melted
2 tablespoons milk

Method:
· Sift the sugars together into a medium-sized bowl.
· Stir the melted butter into the sugar.
· Add milk, mixing well.

Note: If the icing is too thick, you may add a few drops of milk. If it is too thin, let it sit for a while to let the butter solidify. If you need to, you can add more powdered sugar.

CHOCOLATE ICING

YIELD: ICING FOR 1 THREE-LAYER CAKE

*Business is business and
foolishness is foolishness.*

Ingredients:
12 **oz semisweet baking chocolate, chopped**
1 **cup cream**
1 1/2 **cups unsalted butter**
2 1/2 **cups powdered sugar, sifted**
1/2 **teaspoon salt**

Method:
· Combine the chocolate, cream, and butter in a
  saucepan. Cook over low heat until the chocolate
  has melted.
· Remove from heat. Add the sugar, mixing well.
· Allow the mixture to cool, stirring occasionally until it
  reaches spreading consistency.

Coconut Icing

Yield: Icing for 1 three-layer cake

Ingredients:
1/4 **cup all-purpose flour**
1 **cup sugar**
1 **cup milk**
1 **cup butter, softened**
1 **teaspoon vanilla extract**
2 1/2 **cups sweetened shredded coconut**

Method:
- Combine the flour and sugar in a medium saucepan.
- Slowly add the milk. Cook over medium heat, stirring constantly, until the mixture thickens to pudding consistency.
- Remove from the heat and let the mixture cool.
- Add the butter and mix well by hand or with a mixer.
- Add the vanilla extract and 2 cups of the coconut, stirring well.
- Frost the cake. (Icing may need to sit a while to get cool and thick before frosting.)
- After frosting the cake, sprinkle the remaining (1/2 cup) coconut on top.

COCONUT PECAN ICING

YIELD: ICING FOR 1 THREE-LAYER CAKE

Ingredients:
1 **can (12-ounce) evaporated milk**
1 1/2 **cups sugar**
3/4 **cup unsalted butter, softened**
4 **egg yolks, lightly beaten**
1 1/2 **teaspoons vanilla extract**
7 **ounces sweetened shredded coconut**
1/2 **cup chopped pecans**

Method:
- In a saucepan, combine the milk, sugar, butter, and egg yolks. Cook on medium heat, stirring continuously until it is thickened and golden brown.
- Remove from the heat, stir in the vanilla extract, coconut, and pecans.
- Cool until the mixture thickens to a spreading consistency.

CREAM CHEESE ICING

YIELD: ICING FOR 1 THREE-LAYER CAKE

Ingredients:
8 ounces cream cheese, softened
1/2 cup unsalted butter, softened
2 cups powdered sugar
1/4 teaspoon salt
1 teaspoon vanilla extract

Method:
· Beat the cream cheese and butter until smooth.
· Sift the powdered sugar with the salt.
· In several additions, mix the powdered sugar into the cream cheese. Add vanilla.
· Beat until light and fluffy.

Pies, Cobblers,
and Cookies

PIES, COBBLERS, AND COOKIES

PIES
Pie Crust

Apple Pie

Butterscotch Pie

Cherry Pie

Chess Pie

Chocolate Pie

Coconut Cream Pie

Kentucky Pie

Pecan Pie

Lemon Meringue Pie

Pumpkin Pie

Sweet Potato Pie

PUDDINGS AND COBBLER
Banana Pudding

Blackberry Cobbler

COOKIES
Bourbon Balls

Brownies

Cornmeal Cookies

Ginger Cookies

Sugar Cookies

Tea Cakes

When I got babtised, I got babtised in a pool outside the church. I was nine years old. Babtised in the water. Thought I was gonna drown.

I never will forget it, that song that was sung: "Comin' home, comin' home, never more to roam, open wide thine arms of love, Lord, I'm comin' home. I've wandered far away from God, Lord, I'm comin' home. Open wide thine arms of love, Lord, I'm comin' home."

Your babtism's when you join the church. Them was some good ol' songs back then. Oh, yeah!

PIE CRUST

"Put jus' a tiny bit a salt, you know, 'cause it's for the flavor. Somebody said put sugar in it, but I don't. Sugar make it hard, tough-like."

"I never make jus' one crust at a time 'causin' it don't make no sense. Got to make more, then freeze 'em. Somebody always wantin' to get a pie. If you got crusts in the freezer, it don't take no time to make a pie."

YIELD: TWO 9-INCH PIE CRUSTS
ONE DOUBLE 9-INCH PIE CRUST
FOR PREBAKED CRUST: 400° OVEN

Ingredients:
2 **cups all-purpose flour**
1/4 **teaspoon salt**
1/2 **cup solid vegetable shortening**
2 **tablespoons unsalted butter, melted**
1/4 **cup cold water**

Method:
· Sift the flour and salt together.
· Work the shortening into the flour until the dough resembles coarse meal. Rub the shortening and flour together between both hands or use a pastry blender.
· Add the melted butter and work into the dough by hand or with a spoon.
· Add the cold water and work together until just combined. Do not overmix.

Method for single crust pies:
· Divide the dough into two equal portions.
· Roll each portion out into a 10-inch circle about 1/8 inch thick.
· Lift the dough into a 9-inch pie pan. Trim excess dough to the edge of pie pan and flute.

Method for double crust pies:

· Divide dough into two equal portions.

· Roll out the first portion into a 10-inch circle about 1/8 inch thick.

· Lift the dough into a 9-inch pie pan. Trim excess dough to edge of pie pan.

· Roll out the second portion into a 10-inch circle about 1/8 inch thick.

· Cover or wrap dough-lined pie pan and dough for top crust until ready to fill the pie.

· After filling the pie, place second portion of dough on top. Trim dough, to the edge of pie pan. Press edges of dough together and flute.

· Cut slits in top crust to allow steam to escape.

· Follow baking instructions on pie recipe.

Method for prebaked pie crust:

· Using a fork, poke holes all over the bottom of the crust.

· Bake for 8-10 minutes in a 400° oven or until the edges are a deep golden brown. Watch carefully to avoid burning and poke with a fork if crust begins to bubble up.

Method for storage:

Pie crusts freeze very well. They can be frozen baked or unbaked, although unbaked allows the most flexibility. Double wrap in plastic wrap or use zippered freezer bags. For best results use within three months.

APPLE PIE

YIELD: ONE 9-INCH PIE
        425° OVEN

Ingredients:
1 **double pie crust, 9-inch** (see recipe page 132)
5 **medium cooking apples, crisp and tart**
2 **tablespoons butter, melted**
1 **tablespoon lemon juice**
1/2 **cup sugar**
2 **tablespoons all-purpose flour**
1/4 **teaspoon cinnamon**
1/4 **teaspoon nutmeg**

Method:
• Place one crust in the bottom of the pie pan,
  trim excess dough.
• Peel, core, and slice the apples into 1/4-inch wedges.
• Quickly, place the sliced apples in a large bowl and
  gently mix with the melted butter and lemon juice.
• In a small bowl, combine the sugar, flour, and spices.
  Pour over the apples and mix well to combine.
• Arrange the apples in the crust-lined pan so that
  they lie flat.
• Cover with top crust, turn edges under and flute.
  Cut slits in top for steam to escape.
• Bake on the bottom rack of a 350° oven for 45 minutes.
  Move up to the top rack for the last 5-10 minutes to
  brown the crust.

Butterscotch Pie

Yield: One 9-inch pie
400° oven

I don't use no cornstarch in my pies, I don't like the way it tastes. It give a fake flavor — like somethin' artificial. So I use flour for everythin'. I have cornstarch, but I don't never use it. Other folks don't like flour 'cause it makes lumps, but it don't, not the way I make it. Put a little sugar in your flour when you stirrin' it and it won't get lumpy.

Ingredients:
1 **prebaked pie crust, 9-inch** (see recipe page 132)
1/2 **cup all-purpose flour**
1 **cup brown sugar**
1 **cup milk**
3 **eggs, separated**
1/2 **cup unsalted butter**
6 **tablespoons sugar**

Method for filling:
· Make and prebake a 9-inch pie crust.
· Sift the flour and brown sugar into a medium-sized pan.
· Add the milk a little at a time, stirring until well combined.
· Beat the egg yolks, add to the pan and mix.
· Add the butter (in stick form) and cook over medium heat, stirring constantly and making sure the mixture does not stick around the edges.
· Soon after the butter has melted, the pudding will begin to thicken. Continue to stir over medium heat until it gets to pudding consistency.
· Pour into the prebaked pie crust.

Method for meringue:
· Beat the egg whites at medium speed until they are very foamy. Beat at high speed, pausing to add the sugar 1 tablespoon at a time until the mixture forms stiff peaks.
· Spoon the meringue on top of the butterscotch filling. Spread to outer edges and form decorative peaks.
· Bake on the top rack of the oven at 400° for about 4 minutes until the meringue starts to turn golden brown. Watch carefully and rotate pie halfway through browning.

Cherry Pie

"I make this pie on Mr. Washington's birthday, 'causin' he was the one who chopped down the cherry tree and didn't fib about it, neither."

Yield: One 9-inch pie
350° oven

Ingredients:
1 **double pie crust, 9-inch** (see recipe page 132)
1/2 **cup sugar**
1/2 **cup all-purpose flour**
1/2 **teaspoon salt**
1 **teaspoon nutmeg**
1/2 **cup water**
2 **16-ounce cans cherries in syrup**
1/2 **cup unsalted butter**

Method:
- Place one crust in the bottom of the pie pan, trim excess dough.
- Sift the flour, sugar, salt, and nutmeg together into a saucepan and mix well.
- Add water slowly to the flour, stirring constantly.
- Drain the cherries, reserving 1 cup of the syrup.
- Stir the syrup slowly into the flour mixture.
- Add the butter (in stick form) and cook over medium heat, stirring constantly and making sure the mixture does not stick around the edges.
- When the butter melts, the mixture will start to thicken. Take it off the heat when it reaches the consistency of gravy.
- Combine with the cherries and pour into unbaked pie crust.
- Place second portion of dough on top. Trim dough to the edge of pie pan. Press edges of dough together and flute.
- Cut slits in top for steam to escape.
- Bake on the bottom rack of a 350° oven for 25-30 minutes. Move to the top rack for the last 5 to 10 minutes until the crust is golden brown.

CHESS PIE

"When they taste this pie, they won't never want no other kind."

YIELD: ONE 9-INCH PIE
        350° OVEN

Ingredients:

1 **unbaked pie crust, 9-inch (**see recipe page 132**)**

1 **cup sugar**

1/2 **cup butter**

3 **eggs**

1 **tablespoon vanilla extract**

1 **tablespoon white or cider vinegar**

2 **tablespoons yellow cornmeal**

1/2 **teaspoon salt**

Method:

· Make 9-inch pie crust, line pan and flute.

· In a small bowl, cream the butter and sugar together.

· Add the eggs, mixing well. Mix in all the other ingredients.

· Pour the mixture into the unbaked pie crust.

· Bake in the bottom of a 350° oven for 45 minutes or
  until the pie is set. Move to the top rack for the last
  5 minutes to brown the crust.

CHOCOLATE PIE

"I never did make chocolate pie with no measure. Who ever heard of measuring to make a chocolate pie?"

YIELD: ONE 9-INCH PIE
400° OVEN

Ingredients:
1 **prebaked pie crust, 9-inch** (see recipe page 132)
1 **cup sugar**
1/2 **cup all-purpose flour**
1/3 **cup cocoa powder**
1 **cup milk**
3 **eggs, separated**
1/2 **cup unsalted butter**
6 **tablespoons sugar**

Method for filling:
- Make and prebake a 9-inch pie crust.
- Sift the sugar, flour, and cocoa into a medium-sized pan.
- Add the milk a little at a time, stirring until all the ingredients are well combined.
- Beat the egg yolks, add to the pan and mix.
- Add the butter and stir continuously over low to medium heat, making sure to stir around the edges.
- Soon after the butter melts, the pudding will begin to thicken.
- Pour into the prebaked pie shell.

Method for meringue:

- Beat the egg whites on medium speed until they are very foamy.
- Continue to beat at high speed, pausing to add the sugar 1 tablespoon at a time until the mixture forms stiff peaks.
- Spoon the meringue over the chocolate pudding. Spread to outer edges and form decorative peaks.
- Bake on the top rack of a 400° oven for about 4 minutes until the meringue starts to turn golden brown. Watch carefully and rotate the pie halfway through browning.

COCONUT CREAM PIE

YIELD: ONE 9-INCH PIE
400° OVEN

It's a good thing we didn't decide to eat all those pies we done made. We'd be as big as a house. One'd be tryin' to squeeze by the other'n.

Ingredients:
1 **prebaked pie crust, 9-inch** (see recipe page 132)
1/2 **cup all-purpose flour**
1 **cup sugar**
1 **cup milk**
3 **eggs, separated**
1/2 **cup unsalted butter**
2 **cups sweetened shredded coconut**
6 **tablespoons sugar**

Method for filling:
• Make and prebake 9-inch pie crust.
• Sift the flour and sugar into a medium-sized pan.
• Add the milk a little at a time, stirring until well combined.
• Beat the egg yolks, add to the pan and mix.
• Add the butter (in stick form) and cook over medium heat, stirring constantly and making sure the mixture does not stick around the edges.
• Soon after the butter has melted, the pudding will begin to thicken. Continue to stir over medium heat until it gets to pudding consistency.
• Add coconut and mix well.
• Pour into the prebaked pie crust.

Method for meringue:
- Beat the egg whites at medium speed until they are very foamy. Beat at high speed, pausing to add the sugar 1 tablespoon at a time until the mixture forms stiff peaks.
- Spoon the meringue on top of the coconut cream filling. Spread to outer edges and form decorative peaks.
- Bake on the top rack of the oven at 400° for about 4 minutes until the meringue starts to turn golden brown. Watch carefully and rotate pie halfway through browning.

KENTUCKY PIE

YIELD: ONE 9-INCH PIE
350° OVEN

Your pies might jiggle a little bit when you take 'em out. When they cool they settle down.

Ingredients:
1 **unbaked pie crust, 9-inch** (see recipe page 132)
1/2 **cup unsalted butter, softened**
1 **cup sugar**
3 **well-beaten eggs**
1/2 **cup white corn syrup**
1/4 **teaspoon salt**
1 **teaspoon vanilla extract**
3/4 **cup semisweet chocolate chips**
3/4 **cup chopped pecans or english walnuts**
2 **tablespoons bourbon**

Method:
• Make 9-inch pie crust, line pan and flute.
• Cream the butter and sugar together
• Add the eggs and then all the other ingredients. Mix well.
• Pour into the unbaked pie crust.
• Bake in the bottom of a 350° oven for 55 minutes or until the pie is set. Move to the top rack for the last 5 minutes to brown the crust.

Pecan Pie

Yield: One 9-inch pie
350° oven

Ingredients:
1 **unbaked pie crust, 9-inch** (see recipe page 132)
1/2 **cup unsalted butter, melted**
1 **cup brown sugar**
1 **cup corn syrup**
1/4 **teaspoon salt**
3 **eggs, beaten**
1 **teaspoon vanilla extract**
1 1/2 **cup chopped pecans**

Method:
· Make 9-inch pie crust, line pan and flute.
· Combine all the ingredients except the pecans.
· Place the pecans in the unbaked pie crust.
· Pour the liquid mixture over the pecans. (Pecans will float to the top)
· Bake in the bottom of a 350° oven for 55 minutes or until the pie is set. Move to the top rack for the last 5 minutes to brown the crust.

LEMON MERINGUE PIE

YIELD: ONE 9-INCH PIE
400° OVEN

*Your egg whites can be
runny if you don't
whupp'em enough.
Then if you let that
yellow drop in there,
it won't beat no way.
If there's any bit of that
yellow, then it won't
beat. Ain't that funny?*

Ingredients:
1 **prebaked pie crust**, 9-inch (see recipe page 132)
1 **cup sugar**
1/2 **cup all-purpose flour**
1/2 **cup water**
1/2 **cup orange juice**
1/2 **cup lemon juice**
3 **eggs, separated**
1/4 **cup unsalted butter**
6 **tablespoons sugar**

Method for filling:
· Make and prebake a 9-inch pie crust.
· Sift the flour and sugar into a medium-sized pot.
· Add the water, a little at a time, stirring until well combined.
· Add the orange and lemon juice and stir.
· Beat the egg yolks and add to the mixture.
· Add the butter (in stick form, it will melt).
· Cook over low to medium heat, stirring constantly while the butter melts and making sure to get around the edges.
· Soon after the butter has melted, the pudding will begin to thicken.
· Pour into the prebaked pie crust.

Method for meringue:

- Beat the egg whites at medium speed until they are very foamy. Beat at high speed, pausing to add the sugar 1 tablespoon at a time until the mixture forms stiff peaks.
- Spoon the meringue on top of the lemon filling. Spread to outer edges and form decorative peaks.
- Bake on the top rack of the oven at 400° for about 4 minutes until the meringue starts to turn golden brown. Watch carefully and rotate the pie halfway through browning.

PUMPKIN PIE

YIELD: ONE 9-INCH PIE
350° OVEN

The Lord will hear and answer prayers, you jus' gots to be sincere.

Ingredients:
1 **unbaked pie crust, 9-inch** (see recipe page 132)
2 **cups pumpkin** (canned or fresh)
1/2 **cup unsalted butter, melted**
1 **cup sugar**
3 **eggs, beaten**
1/3 **cup milk**
1 **tablespoon all-purpose flour**
1 **teaspoon cinnamon**
1 **teaspoon nutmeg**
1 **teaspoon allspice**

Method:
· Make 9-inch pie crust, line pan and flute.
· In a medium-sized bowl, combine the pumpkin,
  butter, and sugar and mix well.
· Add the beaten eggs and the milk, mixing well.
· Stir in the flour and spices until well combined.
· Pour the mixture into the unbaked pie crust.
· Bake on the bottom rack of a 350° oven for
  25-30 minutes, or until the pie is set. Move to the
  top rack for the last 5 minutes to brown the crust.

Note: If you are using fresh pumpkin, cook, peel, and mash it before making the pie.

SWEET POTATO PIE

YIELD: ONE 9-INCH PIE
350° OVEN

Ingredients:
1 **unbaked pie crust, 9-inch** (see recipe page 132)
1 **large sweet potato**
1/2 **cup unsalted butter, melted**
1 **cup sugar**
3 **eggs, beaten**
1/3 **cup milk**
1 **tablespoon all-purpose flour**
1/4 **teaspoon baking powder**
1 **teaspoon nutmeg**

Method:
• Make 9-inch pie crust, line pan and flute.
• Wash the sweet potato. Cut potato into four pieces.
  Place in a medium-sized pot and cover with water.
  Boil about 30 minutes, until the potatoes are tender .
• Drain, peel and mash.
• In a medium bowl, combine the sweet potato, butter,
  and sugar. Mix well.
• Add the egg and the milk and mix well.
• Stir in the flour, baking powder, and nutmeg until
  well combined.
• Pour the mixture into the unbaked pie shell.
• Bake on the bottom rack of a 350° oven for
  25-30 minutes, or until the pie is set. Move to the
  top rack for the last 5 minutes to brown the crust.

Banana Pudding

Yield: One 8x8-inch pan
400° oven

Ingredients:
1 **cup all-purpose flour**
2 **cups sugar**
2 **cups milk**
4 **eggs, separated**
1/2 **cup butter**
1 **tablespoon vanilla extract**
1 **(12-ounce) package of vanilla wafers**
4 **large bananas**
1/2 **cup sugar**

Method for pudding:
- Sift the flour and 2 cups sugar into a medium-sized pan.
- Beat the egg yolks, add to the pan, and mix.
- Add the butter (in stick form) and cook over low to medium heat, stirring constantly and making sure the mixture does not stick around the edges.
- Soon after the butter has melted, the pudding will begin to thicken. Continue to stir over medium heat until it gets to pudding consistency.
- Remove from the heat and stir in the vanilla extract.

Method for meringue:

- Beat the egg whites on medium speed until they are very foamy. Beat at high speed, pausing to add the sugar one tablespoon at a time until the mixture forms stiff peaks.
- Layer the bottom of an 8x8-inch glass or aluminum pan with some of the vanilla wafers.
- Slice two bananas thin and layer over the vanilla wafers.
- Pour half the pudding over the bananas.
- Make another layer of vanilla wafers, banana slices, and pudding and line the edge of the pan with the last of the wafers.
- Spoon the meringue on top. Spread to outer edges and form decorative peaks.
- Bake on the top rack at 400° for about 4 minutes, until the meringue starts to turn golden brown. Watch carefully and rotate the pudding dish halfway through browning.

BLACKBERRY COBBLER

YIELD: ONE 8x8-INCH COBBLER
350° OVEN

*You can't just up and
quit 'cause something is
all messed up, you got
to stay and help
straighten it out.*

Ingredients for filling:
1/2 **cup unsalted butter**
1/3 **cup water**
2 **cups sugar**
1/4 **cup all-purpose flour**
1/2 **teaspoon nutmeg**
32 **ounces (2 pounds) fresh or frozen blackberries**

Ingredients for top crust:
1 **cup all-purpose flour**
1/4 **teaspoon salt**
1/3 **cup solid vegetable shortening**
2 **tablespoons unsalted butter, melted**
2 **tablespoons cold water**
flour for rolling

Method for filling:
· Melt the butter in a medium-sized pan.
· In a small bowl, mix together the sugar, flour,
  and nutmeg and add this to the butter, stirring
  continuously over medium heat.
· If you are using fresh blackberries, add 1/3 cup
  of water to the pot.
· Add the blackberries, stirring well to combine
  with other ingredients.
· Spoon the mixture into the baking dish.

Method for crust:
- Sift the flour with the salt.
- Work the shortening into the flour until it resembles coarse sand.
- Add the melted butter, working it in a little.
- Add cold water and work the dough together into a ball.
- Using a floured surface, roll the dough out to a thickness of 1/8 inch in a shape larger than the baking dish.
- Lay the dough over the top and trim so that it extends 3/4 inch over the edge. Turn the 3/4 inch of dough under to form a double thickness of crust around the edge. Flute to make a decorative edge.
- Cut vents in the crust to allow steam to escape. Place baking dish on a baking sheet.
- Bake on the bottom rack of a 350° oven for 45-50 minutes, or until the blackberries start to bubble. Move the cobbler to the top rack for the last 8-10 minutes until the crust browns.

Variation:

This recipe will work as well with many other fruits. You may want to adjust the amount of sugar, depending on the tartness of the fruit.

BOURBON BALLS

YIELD: 2 DOZEN

Ingredients:
1 **cup crumbled vanilla wafers**
1 **cup chopped pecans**
1 **cup powdered sugar**
2 **tablespoons unsweetened cocoa**
1/4 **cup bourbon**
1 1/2 **tablespoons corn syrup**
Powdered sugar

Method:
- In a mixing bowl, combine the crumbled vanilla wafer, pecans, sugar, and cocoa. Mix well.
- Combine the bourbon and corn syrup and add to the dry mixture, stirring well to combine.
- Form the mixture into 1-inch balls.
- Roll each of the bourbon balls in powdered sugar.

Note: These freeze well.

BROWNIES

YIELD: 2 DOZEN
325° OVEN

A long time ago my mama tole me, "Where there's a will, there's a way." I didn't know what she was talkin' 'bout back then, but now I do. You got to have the will and the Lord will show you the way.

Ingredients:
8 ounces semisweet chocolate, cut in small pieces
3/4 cup all-purpose flour
1/4 cup unsweetened cocoa
1/2 teaspoon salt
1 cup butter, softened
1 3/4 cups sugar
4 eggs
1 tablespoon vanilla extract
1 cup chopped walnuts

Method:
• Grease a 9x13-inch pan.
• Melt the chocolate in a double boiler, and set aside to cool.
• Sift the flour, cocoa, and salt together. Mix well.
• Cream together the butter and sugar.
• Add the eggs one at a time, mixing well after each.
• Add the vanilla extract and beat until light and fluffy (2-3 minutes).
• Mix in the melted chocolate at low speed.
• Fold in the flour and cocoa mixture by hand with a rubber spatula and mix until well incorporated. Fold in nuts. Do not overmix.
• Spread the mixture evenly in the baking pan.
• Bake in a 325° oven for 35 minutes, or until a toothpick inserted into the center comes out clean but moist.
• Allow the brownies to cool before cutting.

Cornmeal Cookies

Yield: 4 dozen
350° oven

Ingredients:
1 **cup unsalted butter, softened**
1 **cup sugar**
3 **eggs**
1 **teaspoon vanilla extract**
2 **cups all-purpose flour**
1 1/2 **cups yellow cornmeal**
flour for rolling

Method:
· Cream the butter and sugar together until light
  and fluffy.
· Add the eggs one at a time, mixing well after each one.
· Add the vanilla extract and mix well.
· Sift flour and combine with cornmeal.
· Mix in the flour in three additions.
· Divide the dough in half and seal in plastic wrap.
  Refrigerate for an hour or more.
· Unwrap one of the packages of dough and place on a
  floured board. Roll out to a thickness of 1/8 inch.
· Cut with a 2 1/2-inch round biscuit cutter. Place on
  baking sheets. Continue with remaining dough.
· Bake on the middle rack of a 350° oven for 8-10 minutes.

GINGER COOKIES

YIELD: 3 DOZEN
350° OVEN

I feel like shoutin',

I'm so happy

Ingredients:
1/2 **cup unsalted butter**
1 **cup sugar**
1/4 **cup molasses**
2 **eggs**
2 1/2 **cups all-purpose flour**
1/2 **teaspoon baking soda**
1/2 **teaspoon salt**
2 **tablespoons ground ginger**
1 **teaspoon cinnamon**
1 **teaspoon cloves**
flour for rolling

Method:
· Cream the butter and sugar together.
· Add the molasses, mixing well.
· Add the eggs, one at a time, mixing well after each one.
· Sift the flour, salt, baking soda, and spices together.
· Mix in the flour in three additions
· Divide the dough in half and seal in plastic wrap. Refrigerate for an hour or more.
· Unwrap one of the packages of dough and place on a floured board. Roll out to a thickness of 1/8 inch.
· Cut with a 2 1/2-inch round biscuit cutter. Place on baking sheets. Continue with remaining dough.
· Bake on the middle rack of a 350° oven for 8-10 minutes.

SUGAR COOKIES

YIELD: 3 DOZEN
350° OVEN

Ingredients:
1/2 **cup unsalted butter, softened**
3/4 **cup brown sugar**
2 **eggs**
1 **teaspoon vanilla extract**
2 **cups all-purpose flour**
1/2 **teaspoon salt**
flour for rolling

Method:
· Cream the butter and sugar together until light and fluffy.
· Add the eggs, one at a time, mixing well after each one.
· Add the vanilla extract and mix well.
· Sift the flour and salt together.
· Add flour to the butter mixture a little at a time, mixing well after each addition.
· Divide the dough in half, and seal in plastic wrap. Refrigerate for an hour or more.
· Unwrap one of the packages of dough and place on a floured board. Roll out to a thickness of 1/8 inch.
· Cut with a 2 1/2-inch round biscuit cutter. Place on baking sheets 1 inch apart. Continue with remaining dough.
· Bake on the middle rack of a 350° oven for 8-10 minutes.

TEA CAKES

"We'd be in the field and my grandmomma would cook up them tea cakes and come out there holdin' an umbrella over 'em. She had a whole basket of 'em."

"I make 'em up like I make biscuits. Sugar, butter, flour, flavor, egg— and mix it all up together. Roll it out and cut 'em."

YIELD: 2 1/2 DOZEN
350° OVEN

Ingredients:
1 **cup unsalted butter, softened**
1 **cup sugar**
3 **eggs, beaten**
1 **teaspoon vanilla extract**
3 1/2 **cups all-purpose flour**
1/2 **teaspoon salt**
flour for rolling

Method:
· Cream the butter and sugar together until light and fluffy.
· Add the eggs, one at a time, mixing well after each.
· Add the vanilla extract and mix well.
· Sift the flour with salt. Mix in the flour in three additions.
· Turn half the mixture out onto a well floured board and roll out to a thickness of 1/2 inch. Dough will be wet, so use as much flour as you need to keep it from sticking.
· Cut with a 2 1/2-inch round biscuit cutter. Place on baking sheets 1 inch apart. Roll and cut remaining dough.
· Bake in a 350° oven for 15 minutes, or until the edges begin to turn golden brown.

I can do all things through Christ which strenghteneth me.

PHILIPPIANS 4:13

Photographic Credits

Front cover food photo—Bernard Kane

Front cover portrait photo of Annie Johnson—
photographer unknown; Photo retouching by Asha McLaughlin

Back cover photo—John Lair

Photo page 5 (birthday party)—photographer unknown; taken in
the basement of Mrs. Taylor's house at a birthday party for
Annie's granddaughter Anna Louise Patterson.

Photo page 8 (front porch)—Tom Rankin; taken on Annie's front
porch on Vermont Avenue in the late 70's.

Photo page 17—John Lair, the famous Easy-Bake Oven.

Photo page beginning of Annie Lee Section—John Lair

Photo at the beginning of Annie's Recipes and all other
sections—Bernard Kane.

Colophon

Book Design—David Hartman Designs, Inc.

Printing and Binding—Thomson-Shore, Inc.

Typefaces—*Mrs Eaves* by Emigre Fonts

Composed on a Apple Power Macintosh 7600/132
using QuarkXpress 3.3

Paper—60# Supple Opaque (recycled)

HOW TO REACH US

If you would like an additional copy of this book,
please check with your bookstore or call:
1-800-710-8551

or write to:
Grace Publishers
P.O. Box 769
S. Fallsburg, NY 12779

or e-mail:
GracePubl@aol.com
or visit our website:
www.gracepublishers.com

Art Ableman, Stephanie Altobellis, Christell Anderson, Robert Atkins, Acha Bailey, Victoria Bailey, Dorothy Baldwin, Diana Beaumont, Lotie Beecham, Hattie Benford, Lonnie Benford, Michele Bessler, Mark Besten, Christian Boy, Shirley Bradshaw, Howard Braunstein, Cecy Brewer, McHenry Brewer, Marshall Bridgewaters, Douglas Brooks, Mrs. Brooks, Eugene Callender, Cynthia Cannon, Dana Cannon, Katherine Cannon, Martin Cannon, Kathleen Cano, Amanda Carter, Addie Cartwright, Sherry Cartwright, Rafe Cecil, Mrs. Cloud, Reverend C. C. Cloud, Hiram Cody III, Martha Neal Cooke, Audrey Couloumbis, Neil Davidson, Erin Delaney, Fran Delaney, Juney Delaney, Frank D'Autilia, Jeanne D'Autilia, John DeNicolo, Lou D'Andrea, Gene Douglas, Louise Douglas, Mike Dove, Patty Dove, John Downey, Arnold Drogen, Jacky Durnell, Mary Eitel, Ellenville National Bank, Kathleen Ellis, Paul Ellis, Ruthie Ervin, Bud Ewing, Caroline Ewing, Ann Fleming, Dennis Fleming, JoAnn Fleming, Ken Fleming, Katherine Fleming, Joan Foret, Breton Frazier, Hank Friedman, Tim Fuller, Rob Gardiner, Paige Gettinger, Kathryn Gillett, Bob Girton, Reiko Gomez, Grace Magnolia, Eddie Grady, Annie Green, Jonathan Greene, Bill Groth, Dayna Halprin, Patty Halprin, Robert Halprin, Sarah Halprin, Susie Hammer, David Hammer, Sandra Hampton, Susan Hardy, David Hartman, Mary Hartman, Lisa Hashman, Mark Helm, Michele Higgins, Pamela Howard, Michael Hunt, Stacey Irvin, Pamela Jefferson,